a

Sagar

VOLUME SEVEN

With kind regards, ॐ and prem

Swami Niranjan

Bhakti Yoga Sagar

(Ocean of the Yoga of Devotion)

Swami Satyananda Saraswati

Satsangs at Sri Panch Dashnam Paramahamsa Alakh Bara, Rikhia, Deoghar, during Sita Kalyanam, from 11–19 December 2001.

VOLUME SEVEN

Yoga Publications Trust, Munger, Bihar, India

Published by Yoga Publications Trust
   First edition 2002

ISBN: 81-86336-28-1
Price: Indian rupees one hundred only

Publisher and distributor: Yoga Publications Trust, Ganga Darshan, Munger, Bihar, India.

Website: www.yogavision.net
E-mail: ypt@yogavision.net

Printed at Thomson Press (India) Limited, New Delhi, 110001

SWAMI SIVANANDA SARASWATI

Swami Sivananda was born at Patta-madai, Tamil Nadu, in 1887. After serving as a medical doctor in Malaya, he renounced his practice, went to Rishikesh and was initiated into Dashnami sannyasa in 1924 by Swami Vishwananda Saraswati. He toured extensively throughout India, inspiring people to practise yoga and lead a divine life. He founded the Divine Life Society at Rishikesh in 1936, the Sivananda Ayurvedic Pharmacy in 1945, the Yoga Vedanta Forest Academy in 1948 and the Sivananda Eye Hospital in 1957. During his lifetime Swami Sivananda guided thousands of disciples and aspirants all over the world and authored over 200 books.

SWAMI SATYANANDA SARASWATI

Swami Satyananda was born at Almora, Uttar Pradesh, in 1923. In 1943 he met Swami Sivananda in Rishikesh and adopted the Dashnami sannyasa way of life. In 1955 he left his guru's ashram to live as a wandering mendicant and later founded the International Yoga Fellowship in 1963 and the Bihar School of Yoga in 1964. Over the next 20 years Swami Satyananda toured internationally and authored over 80 books. In 1987 he founded Sivananda Math, a charitable institution for aiding rural development, and the Yoga Research Foundation. In 1988 he renounced his mission, adopting kshetra sannyasa, and now lives as a paramahamsa sannyasin.

SWAMI NIRANJANANANDA SARASWATI

Swami Niranjanananda was born at Rajnandgaon, Madhya Pradesh, in 1960. At the age of four he joined the Bihar School of Yoga and was initiated into Dashnami sannyasa at the age of ten. From 1971 he travelled overseas and toured many countries for the next 11 years. In 1983 he was recalled to India and appointed President of Bihar School of Yoga. During the following 11 years he guided the development of Ganga Darshan, Sivananda Math and the Yoga Research Foundation. In 1990 he was initiated as a paramahamsa and in 1993 anointed preceptor in succession to Swami Satyananda. Bihar Yoga Bharati was founded under his direction in 1994. He has authored over 20 books and guides national and international yoga programs.

SWAMI SATYASANGANANDA SARASWATI

Swami Satyasangananda (Satsangi) was born on 24th March 1953, in Chandorenagore, West Bengal. From the age of 22 she experienced a series of inner awakenings which led her to her guru, Swami Satyananda. From 1981 she travelled ceaselessly with her guru in India and overseas and developed into a scholar with deep insight into the yogic and tantric traditions as well as modern sciences and philosophies. She is an efficient channel for the transmission of her guru's teachings. The establishment of Sivananda Math in Rikhia is her creation and mission, and she guides all its activities there, working tirelessly to uplift the weaker and underprivileged areas. She embodies compassion with clear reason and is the foundation of her guru's vision.

Contents

Introduction 1

Satsang One 8

       Two 12

       Three 26

       Four 37

       Five 46

       Six 57

       Seven 67

       Eight 80

       Nine 90

       Ten 100

       Eleven 108

       Twelve 117

       Thirteen 128

       Fourteen 146

       Fifteen 162

Glossary 189

Index 195

Introduction

The Sat Chandi Maha Yajna at Rikhia in 2001 attracted thousands of people from all parts of the world. It meant so many things to so many people. The magnanimity of the event was awesome. The multitudes of people, the diversity of events, the profundity of the sacred rituals, the participation of people from so many different nationalities, religions, and diverse classes, colours and creeds, the enrapturing melodies and mantras all blended perfectly with each other.

But above all it was the uninterrupted presence of Swami Satyananda that added the final touch to the event by giving it a spiritual vibrancy that was unmatched. One can certainly say that apart from attracting thousands of people, the yajna also attracted the divine forces to grace us with their luminous presence. The smoothness, ease and splendour with which it was carried out only points a finger in that direction. No human effort could have made it so attractive.

The most significant part of the yajna was the sankalpa of Rajasooya Yajna made by Sri Swamiji. After twelve years of rigorous and arduous panchagni and allied sadhanas, which he commenced in 1990, Sri Swamiji inaugurated the Rajasooya Yajna and said that it will continue for the next twelve years. The only difference is that he did panchagni in

1

total isolation whereas the Rajasooya Yajna will be done in the presence of everyone, with their participation and involvement.

The Rajasooya is a yajna which can be held only by a *chakravarti,* or one who is recognized as a conqueror. Ordinarily when we speak of conquest we attribute it to territories, kingdoms and countries. But this is not necessarily so. One who conquers the world through an idea, a thought or a philosophy can also be proclaimed a chakravarti.

A conqueror of hearts is a chakravarti too. Sri Rama performed the Rajasooya Yajna. Krishna, although he was a conqueror in every sense of the word, did not. He did preside over the Rajasooya Yajna held by Yudhishthira though, which became famous mainly because at this yajna Krishna washed the feet of all the guests and the plates as well.

As it is the custom for a chakravarti to declare what he has conquered, Sri Swamiji pronounced that fixing the flag of yoga in all corners of the world was his conquest. To take yoga out of the caves of hermits and present it to the people in a manner most beneficial to them was also a conquest. Although he did not say this, we all know that to make it useful for society and mankind was solely his conquest. No wonder then that he found a place in their hearts also. When you uplift others you find a place in their hearts as well.

There was a time when yajnas were a part of the day to day culture of this land. Rishis and munis performed yajnas of all kinds. It was quite common to drop in at the hermitage of a rishi and discover them in the midst of a yajna. The chanting of Vedic mantras abounded in the atmosphere. The fragrance of homa and the tranquil resonance of sattwic vibrations filled the air. It felt as if beauty and auspiciousness had made their permanent abode there. The seasons were always kind and benevolent. Fruits and flowers adorned the trees. Birds chirped merrily. Deer and wild beasts frolicked around, not at all wary of humans. The water and air was pure and invigorating. Peace and tranquillity pervaded the surroundings.

Imagine that picturesque scene – the simplicity and richness of that event; the surcharged energy and feeling of unity that it generates; the willpower and stamina that it creates; the immense satisfaction and joy that is felt; the dynamism and power of the mantras which forbid any negative vibrations to enter that sphere; the love and compassion that arises from within; the profound understanding that develops of the role of each and every speck of creation and one's own place within that.

That is the purpose of a yajna. Yajna is no different to yoga. Asanas, pranayama, dharana and dhyana are not the only forms of yoga. Yajna is also a form of yoga. Asanas discipline and regulate the body to function in its optimum condition. Dharana and dhyana train the mind to focus and concentrate. Those forms of yoga are for the body and mind, the physical attributes of man. Yajnas are more than that, they are esoteric yoga. They deal with a part of you that you do not know, have never experienced and can never see. Yajnas communicate with the hidden part of you. It is not the language of words, it is pure experience. Therefore, your conscious mind cannot understand it nor is it even necessary for your mind to comprehend all that is happening.

The mind simply does not have the faculty to know that dimension because it functions in the realm of intelligence. Even your *buddhi,* the discriminating aspect of mind, cannot take you there because buddhi is governed by intellect. Beyond intelligence and intellect there is a much greater power and that is intuition or *prajna.* Yajnas alter the state of mind and buddhi to give an experience of that. The esoteric nature of a yajna draws out eternal archetypes that are embedded in us. Without our knowledge, with ease and comfort great transformations take place within us. Samskaras from the causal body get a chance to express themselves and thus blockages and obstacles are removed.

Yajnas exist in time as well as beyond time and space. The smoke that arises from the yajna kund travels to higher realms and other planes of existence. It is consumed by the

3

cosmic energy. This is why yajnas are conducted by proficient pandits with great accuracy and philosophical attention.

Everything that is offered at a yajna is taken from nature. No substances of chemical or artificial origin are used. The fuel that is burnt is aromatic and purifies the air. It is kindled by rubbing the samidha sticks, not with a candle or matchstick. The people who kindle the fire are those who have been devoted to fire worship for generations and generations. In their daily life they worship the fire with mantras at sunrise and sunset. It is called the heavenly fire because it reaches out to the heavens and forms a link between heaven and earth.

This enchanting scene is recreated at Paramahamsa Alakh Bara during Sita Kalyanam. It gives us a chance to witness the glorious heritage bestowed on us by our ancestors, the rishis and munis. It is such events that restore global order and uphold the world we live in. If yajnas were not held the earth would degenerate and all life would be crushed. We would not have to die to go to hell, we would experience it here while living.

Yajna is not just ritual. Just to light a fire and chant some mantras is not yajna. It is much more than that. To make a yajna efficacious and derive all of its benefits, one has to pour one's heart and soul into it. This is why yajnas performed by rishis, munis and enlightened saints are very dynamic and powerful. Because they alone can accomplish the total projection of oneself that a yajna demands. It is as if life is poured into the yajna by their very presence.

In this twenty-first century, when global order has been replaced by global disorder, performing yajnas becomes an act of greater importance in order to restore harmony. This is not religion, it is knowledge of life and how to live. This is not a religious observance to invoke some gods and god-desses. It is the process through which you can know yourself and converse with your inner being. It is a chance to fulfil the aim of human life, which is to realize one's own Self.

Performance of a yajna is an act of universal love and compassion – universal because it is not limited. It reaches

4

out to all that is animate and inanimate, the manifest as well as the unmanifest. It is an act of love because it expresses our remembrance of that which gave us life and gratitude for the chance to live. It is an act of repaying a debt to Nature for feeding and nurturing us on this beautiful earth, and an unspoken thanks for all that we have received from it. This is true compassion, to give back what you have received. This heightened remembrance in return re-nourishes us and gives us the ability to achieve our objectives and goals with ease and splendour. Thus our relationship with existence grows deeper and deeper and the bonds strengthen more and more.

There are three aspects to a yajna. If one of these three aspects is missing the yajna is incomplete. The first is the ritual itself, which consists of adorning the area of the yajna, invocation of higher forces through the chanting of mantras, kindling of the fire and offering of oblations into it. The second is satsang or association with sadhus and saints. To listen to the Truth is satsang. To be in the presence of Truth is satsang. To be able to withstand Truth is satsang. This is a vital part of the yajna. The third is daan. *Daan* means to give away what belongs to you. A yajna without daan is like a newly married bride without ornaments. The act of daan glorifies a yajna. It is the cream on top of the pudding. Offerings at a yajna earn thousand-fold merits in this life and hereafter.

Daan does not mean charity and alms alone. When you offer a gift or present to someone who is not in need, that too is daan. To give something to someone in need is charity. To give to one who is not in need is a gift. Kings and emperors also received daan in abundance from rishis during yajnas. Not just the poor but each and every person at a yajna is eligible for daan. It is the prasad of the yajna.

The act of yajna is so attractive because it is pure and simple. It is in harmony with Nature and its creation. Purity and simplicity are essential ingredients of a yajna. In order to maintain the purity and simplicity, yajnas evolved into a highly technical science. Just as modern day scientists evolved matter to create highly technical missiles and satellites, in the same way the sophisticated and refined science of yajna also creates a laser guided missile which does not just remain restricted to this realm but travels far beyond. The only difference is that the yajna missile is composed of love and compassion and not of hatred and destruction. It is a benevolent missile and not a malevolent one. This missile creates, not destroys. It rejuvenates, not extinguishes.

Yajna is an act of bhakti or pure devotion. It is uncontaminated power which is known to perform miracles, alter events, nullify calamities, make the blind see, the deaf hear, the lame walk and the mute speak. In bhakti there is no room for doubt. How hard it is to have bhakti for something you have never seen. Bhakti rests on faith. Faith that what you have not seen is there close beside you taking care of you with each breath.

According to most ancient traditions recorded in the life of Rama, the speciality of the Rajasooya Yajna is perfection in the art of giving. It was thus understood that only emperors and chakravartis could undertake this yajna and it was named rajasooya, as *raja* means one who governs. Who else but a raja can give with an open and joyous heart.

This art of giving is known as *bhet*. Bhet is not just about giving, it is about receiving as well. Rather it is receiving and returning what you have received after adding to it a touch of excellence. So you always get back in abundance what you give. In the first year of the Rajasooya Yajna, Sri Swamiji offered to all, including hundreds and thousands of families from Rikhia and neighbouring panchayats, *vastra* or cloth brought from all parts of India. In 2002, the second year, his offering of bhet will be *patra*, which in this context means container, vessel or utensil.

The giving exemplified in the Rajasooya Yajna is a total giving which extends from the material to the spiritual. By such a chakravarti, along with vastra, patra and anna (grain), both jnana and bhakti can also be given as bhet. But just as in a yoga class it has to be graded, not just all at once.

There is an adage in Hindi which, when translated, means that your patra or vessel can hold only as much as the capacity it is used to. Through implication it tells us that in order to receive more you will have to enlarge your vessel. This is only possible through giving. So come to the Rajasooya Yajna and learn the art of giving and receiving.

Satsang 1

December 9, 2001

God's name is a very high potency dose. You only need to sing God's name a little. Just as you don't add a cup of sugar to a cup of tea or a kilo of salt to a kilo of vegetables, in the same way you don't need to sing God's name a lot of times. God's name is like sugar, salt or hot chilli – a little is enough. If you overdo it there will be problems. So just sing God's name a little and enjoy it. If it works for you it can transport you immediately, it can tele-transport you.

Polytheism leads to tolerance

Polytheism results in a very tolerant and enduring society. Polytheism is a philosophical principle and system, but its effect on world politics is tolerance. Monotheism is also a philosophical system and principle, but the effect is in-tolerance. In monotheism there is only one God, but in polytheism there are many gods. Therefore, monotheistic religions are very intolerant; they say, "This is the only way." Polytheism says, "This is the way; that is also the way. Your way is also the way." Every room, every building, every house has its own entrance. The path that leads to my house cannot lead to your house.

So, remember that in India we have accepted polytheism with a far reaching and broad world vision. You must

8

remember that. It is not a religion that I am teaching, it is a system of society for humankind. God is indefinable. You can't define Him as one. One is not one, one is infinity. Because if God is one, then one plus one is two. But if God is infinity, that one plus one is equal to one, one minus one is equal to one – *poornamadah poornamidam*. That is the meaning.

Theme song

The theme song for this year is "I am Thy servant, O Lord." It begins,

Ai maalik tere bande ham,
Aise ho hamaare karam,
Nekee par chale aur badi se tale,
Taaki haste hue nikale dam.

This song is known to all Indians. As all languages are God's languages we have had the theme song translated into English. The group leaders from the different countries will translate it into their languages – Greek, German, French, Slavic and so on. Everyone can then understand the meaning when they are singing. The rehearsal for this theme song will take place today and tomorrow and it will be put to use at the invocation ceremony of Devi. We will offer this submission before Her to seek Her gracious blessings. Without that our minds cannot be corrected. The meaning of the prayer is,

I am Thy servant, O Lord,
Guide my karmas well
To choose the correct path,
And perform only those actions that avert evil
So that when I leave my body it is with a smile.

The glow of contentment is fast disappearing
And dense darkness is spreading all around.
The man you have created is worried, anxious
and out of gear
with no hope in sight.

9

The power of your radiance alone
can transform the dark night
into the luminosity of the full moon.

Help me, O Lord, to keep my balance
when I face injustice and atrocities,
And give me the strength not to seek revenge
but to stick to good deeds,
Even when others harm me,
So that the love within me grows
and differences and delusions disappear.

This man is very weak
and still full of millions of shortcomings,
Despite which this earth on which we live
does not fall apart
because of the grace which You shower on it.
We too are Your creation and seek Your assistance,
love and forgiveness
To absorb our sorrows.

Guide my karmas well
To choose the correct path,
And perform only those actions that avert evil
So that when I leave my body it is with a smile.

The situation existing in the world today is really pathetic as nothing is within our control. We are controlled by external forces. Parents have no control over their sons or daughters. When you are not in control of your own mind, how can you control your offspring? You want to control yourselves and to do that many of you take a vow in the evening, but by morning it has evaporated. I pondered over this situation and thought, let us seek succour from the Almighty. When even the gods begged the Almighty to get rid of the demon Ravana, why not seek His blessings to get rid of the Ravana existing within us and in society?

So, our theme song is in tune with the situation prevailing in and around us: "O my Lord, we are helpless though we are Your servants..." The prayer is to God so that He will accomplish everything for us. God does not go into details. He just understands your feelings. God is like a child. So even if you don't understand the meaning of the prayer, if you just feel, "God, I am helpless, help me," that's enough. A little baby cries. He doesn't say, "Mummy, I want milk." He says, "Aaah! Aaah!" and Mummy comes. It is the *bhavana*, the emotion, the real feeling that comes. Although the baby may just be crying and not even asking for milk, still the mother somehow understands he needs milk. So, it's not that we are asking God to do something, but that He should understand what we need today. This is the right time in this present age of Kali Yuga for a divine power to descend and set to right everything that is wrong.

Satsang 2

December 10, 2001

Swami Niranjan: Do you intend to have a glimpse of God? If so, you will need to be disciplined during this program. No one has come here for entertainment or a tea party. Those who have come for that purpose should ponder this. People have come here to participate in the yajna, to be a part and parcel of this sacred yajna. The yajna being performed here is of special significance. You may have seen other yajnas performed in India, in villages and cities, but this yajna, which is being performed under the guidance of Sri Swamiji, is most sacred and the whole environment here is most disciplined. Hence you have to participate with that discipline in mind from morning to evening.

Devi's grace requires discipline
You will recall that during last year's yajna, Sri Swamiji told you to come fully prepared for this year's yajna. You should not smoke. A person who is habituated to smoking will not be satisfied with just one or two cigarettes, but will regularly increase the number. Such a person will not be satisfied with smoking and will go out for tea, coffee and other things. So, those of you who are habituated to these things in your homes and offices need not do that here. It is not acceptable and not permitted. You must be aware that if you do not

12

strictly follow the discipline of the yajna, you will not be able to receive the benefit of this yajna. You will lose your prasad from the Mother Goddess too. Sri Swamiji has kindly allowed Devi's prasad to be bestowed upon everyone from this year. You will be called only once to receive the prasad and if you are not here to receive it, your turn will not come again, and the loss of Devi's grace will be yours.

Furthermore, only if you can remain present here, physically and mentally, will you be able to grasp what is happening. If you want to have the gracious blessings of Devi, if you desire to have peace and opulence in your life, then you need to follow the discipline required for such sacred grace. No one receives Devi's grace without that discipline. If you follow the rules of the yajna strictly, then Devi's grace will reach you in abundance. When you opt for a government job, first of all you study hard, obtain a degree, apply in the job market and wait in the queue for an interview. But if you leave the line and go to the toilet, your name may be called out and you may lose the opportunity of getting that job. In your absence, the next in line will get the opportunity and go ahead of you. So, if you want to receive something precious, you will have to follow the rules of the game. You will have to strive hard, otherwise you will be a loser. I am telling you this for your own benefit. To follow it or not is your choice.

Yajna – tool for change

Sri Swamiji: Yajna is a very powerful tool. It includes the body, the mind, faith, mantra, ritual as well as your entire life. The combination of all these makes yajna a very, very powerful tool of metamorphosis, transformation and change. If you forget to put salt in the dal, it will not have the desired taste even if you add groundnut, saffron or turmeric. In the same way, this type of yajna requires total commitment and coordination. The body, the mind and the mantras all unite to produce a special effect which changes your thinking and your life. You will have to understand what life is when this total participation takes place. The effect of the yajna becomes

13

very, very powerful. A yajna like this is a massive and effective process. It is a scientific process which includes a most important thing – faith. You were born with faith. You did not get it from your university, nor did you get it from your religion or from your society. You came with faith from your mother's womb. This faith is very powerful and can accomplish great things in life.

You have been drinking tea all your life and can continue to do so in the future. There is no harm in it as the tea that you drink is also one of God's creations, in the same way as cigarettes, wine and fish are His creations. Human beings may use them, but some sort of restraint is necessary during these sacred occasions. That is what Swami Niranjan was emphasizing. You can smoke. Who cares? Drink, eat meat, enjoy life because that's your right. There is nothing wrong with enjoying life. Live the way you wish. If you want to smoke cigars or drink champagne, then do it. But there is a time when you have to abstain, and these nine days are the right time. So tighten your nuts and bolts. This is the first point.

Rajasooya Yajna
The second point is about the yajna. This yajna is a mini Rajasooya Yajna. The maxi or big one we will do in the future. For now be a participant in this mini Rajasooya Yajna. What is this Rajasooya Yajna? When a king returned after achieving victory over his counterparts and contemporaries, he would perform the Rajasooya Yajna. I have also had victory throughout the world, but of a different type. I did not vanquish my contemporaries with the sword. Rather I established yoga throughout the world when very few people knew about it. I unfurled the flag of yoga in all countries, islands and continents, among people of all religions and faiths, and everyone bowed down to my flag of yoga. No one dared to oppose me. It is because of this victory of mine that this Rajasooya Yajna is being performed.

When I started preaching yoga in India and elsewhere, the world was not at all aware of yoga. Wherever I went I preached yoga in my own humble, inimitable way. I don't believe in a high profile personality. No! I went in my own way to the ordinary people of India, Australia, England and other countries. I didn't have any flirtations with prime ministers or governors or ambassadors or film stars. I don't believe in that even now. This world is made up of ordinary people like you. We are all common people, we are the masses. Someone works in a factory, someone else is an engineer or a doctor, another is a labourer or a gardener, a shoemaker or a blacksmith. That is what Christ also did. I lived with the people right around the world from here to South America. I established the kingdom of yoga and I consider myself a conqueror. It is to celebrate that victory that this mini Rajasooya Yajna is beginning.

We discuss spiritual matters here. You give to me and I give to you. In this mini Rajasooya Yajna, everyone who comes will receive something, either a dhoti, a sari, a lengha, an angavastra or an ornament. I will give you something, which is called prasad, and you will also give me something. In the maxi or big Rajasooya Yajna, which will be held in the future, from sunrise to sunset everyone will be fed sumptuously – brahmins, kshatriyas, Christians, Hindus, Muslims, cattle, roosters, hens, chickens, pigs, birds, buffaloes, donkeys and horses. Everyone will be fed from dawn to dusk.

This yajna was performed by the Emperor Yudhishthira in his capital at Indraprastha. Later Sri Rama performed the same yajna. Such a yajna is always associated with *digvijaya*, victory over all continents. We are sannyasins. A sannyasin does not hold a *rajadanda*, the weapon of a ruler. A sannyasin holds a *yogadanda,* the flagstaff of yoga. Yogadanda, not rajadanda, is our subject. Lord Buddha also established himself in many countries. It is possible that he also might have performed some sort of yajna. Now I am performing this sacred yajna.

Earrings from God
It is God's wish that this year the married women of this panchayat will receive two big earrings, or *jhumakas*. A thought

15

process had been going on in my mind as to what to give the womenfolk during Sita Kalyanam. One day I heard a cassette tape being played in an adjoining village. The song was, *"Jhumaka gira re, Bareilly ke bazaar mein."* It is a funny song. It means, "Somebody dropped their earrings in the market of Bareilly." Bareilly is in Uttar Pradesh. I didn't understand the meaning. I asked Swami Satsangi what a jhumaka was because I am not familiar with these ornaments. She said that jhumakas were long earrings of silver or gold.

Immediately I resolved to distribute jhumakas to all the women and girls of this panchayat. I thought, "Now God wants me to give earrings to married women. Oh my God! In India there are so many married women! I will have to make a choice. In the panchayat where I live there may be two or three thousand married women." The same day a traveller from Gorakhpur offered me three thousand pairs of jhumakas.

Just see how things happen. God works through us. He works through anyone because He is in everyone's heart. God resides in your heart so every one of you will get your prasad. God works through his Yogamaya. She is private secretary to God. He directed Yogamaya to give this idea to Swami Satyananda. Even through a tape recorder God gave me the message that earrings had fallen in the Bareilly market. This is the market of Bareilly!

The song continues to float in the air. The original song gives me immense pleasure. In the film version the rhythm and metre have been changed and only the meaning is original. In the villages even on the occasion of Satya Narayana pooja cassettes of film songs are played. The rural folk are very simple. They can hardly distinguish between film songs and devotional songs. On the one hand worship of Satya Narayana goes on, and on the other a film song is played. I love singing and dancing. I have audiocassettes of Michael Jackson, George Harrison, John Lennon, Pandit Jasraj and Jagjeet Singh. I have a collection of many different kinds of songs.

Change of perspective

I have not invited you all here for entertainment of the type you find when you go to a hill station or an amusement park. For such things the world is before you. You require a change of perspective and thinking here. If your clothes are still dirty even after having been washed with detergent, then there must necessarily be something wrong with the detergent. But the simile may not be that important because when you are at a solemn and sacred place like a yajna of this magnitude, you are very near to God and so your thought process and behaviour must change. If, after participating in this yajna, even one of your bad traits is removed, then surely you are on the right path. A change for the better in your thinking would lead you to greater heights and change the future of mankind.

Destiny, purushartha and God's grace

Every one of us has a fate, a destiny. You can call it by different names, but it becomes the basis for all the pain and pleasure that we have to undergo. It is responsible for poverty or riches, hope or despair, having a son or a daughter, remaining childless or having offspring. No one strives for sorrow, misery or pain. No one makes an effort to live in poverty or sickness. Everyone strives for a happy, healthy and prosperous life, for success in service, business and commerce, and yet one fails to get it. Why? It proves that there was something beyond human effort, which you may call *prarabdha karma*, the karma determining one's present life. Is prarabdha karma or destiny dependent on *purushartha*, self-effort? This is both my question and answer to you. Are man's achievements the outcome of his destiny or his purushartha? Our seers say God's grace. In short when God's grace is received, no one has to do any purushartha.

Destiny or purushartha are both useless in comparison to God's grace. To receive that grace, our seers say, requires complete faith in God. This is why I have instructed you all to remain present during this yajna. Let your faith in God be so deep that you submerge yourself fully in Him in such

17

a way that sorrow is transformed into happiness. Despair goes and hope comes. Sorrow and pain are like day and night; they come and go, continually changing their positions like a rotating wheel. This is a fact. Hence, let there be some changes in your life to experience God's grace, the ultimate divine grace. Each one of us must try to obtain it.

Divine grace is the ultimate answer to all our problems. To obtain divine grace is my reason for calling you here. In Rikhia I have received many things. I may not be able to tell you what I got and how I got it, but I must convey to you that this is a very good place. You can spend even four or five days here and if you can submerge yourself in the name of God, if your mind can centre around Him, you will definitely know what I got here and how I got it.

God is in you

How to feel the presence of God all the time? You feel the presence of your friends, your children, your pain, your worries and your problems all the time, but you do not know how to feel the presence of God. In fact, you are not even able to feel your own presence, because He is in you. He is not outside you. Swami Sivananda used to sing,

> *In earth, water, fire, air and ether is Ram.*
> *In the heart, mind, prana and senses is Ram.*
> *In the breath, blood, nerves and brain is Ram.*
> *In sentiment, thought, word and action is Ram.*
> *Within is Rama, without is Ram, in front is Ram.*
> *Above is Ram, below is Ram, behind is Ram.*
> *To the right is Ram, to the left is Ram,*
> *Everywhere is Ram.*
> *Ram, Ram, Ram, Ram, Ram, Ram.*

The divine is worshipped in the form of shakti. God in the form of the eternal presence, God in the form of omnipresence, is everywhere, but why don't we feel Him? I know a lot about the subject. I've written books and spoken about it at length. I have done a lot of japa, lakhs and crores of japa. I have done a lot of mantra writing. I have visited all the pilgrimage places, but I did not know how to have the divine presence I was aware that there is something called the divine presence, but I did not know how to have it. Even today, I don't know how to have it – but I have it.

I was aware of the fact that God's presence can be experienced in the same way that we experience the spirit, or the presence of fear, animosity or lust. I knew God's presence throughout just as a woman thinks and feels about a man or a man feels about a woman. I tried to experience Him in different ways. For that I moved straight and also obliquely, spoke for hours about Him, wrote book after book, but the path leading to Him remained far away from me. I used to ponder over which way to go to Him. Whichever path I trod I found His door locked and barred. But now I experience Him. Why I have this experience now I can't explain. But when I experience His presence only He remains in my vision. And then I recall Kabir's words, in which he said, "When I was present, He was not, and now when He is present and visible, I am not there." Because in His presence this differentiation between Him and me is completely obliterated.

Purpose of life
The experience of God is very precious and it is the ultimate truth of human life. Why is there a human incarnation? Why is a donkey or a dog born? Why does a snake incarnate? Why does a human incarnate? What is nature's purpose in creating and evolving the human body? Precisely for manifesting the unmanifest God. Man has been given this body to realize the invisible God as a visible power. Understand this clearly, because man is the only creature who can think about God and proceed towards Him. The rest of the eighty-four lakh species of creation, like dogs, cats, elephants, horses and so on, are engaged in eating, drinking, sleeping and procreation.

It has been clearly stated that as far as the basic instincts are concerned, humans and animals are similar. The only difference is that humans think, sing in praise of the Lord and reach Him through perseverance and bhakti, devotion. The only difference between animals and us is that we can experience God. We are aware of God. We are searching for Him. We have questions about Him. Let us think, therefore, that this time in Rikhia is the right opportunity to maintain this God consciousness as much as possible.

Yajna – a process of life

Swami Niranjan: Sri Swamiji has mentioned many times that yajna is a process that generates, propagates and culminates. Yajna is the process of life: life is generated, life is nurtured and life is destroyed. Yajna is not a fire ceremony, although the fire ceremony, the mantras and the other invocations which invoke the deity in symbolic form are part of it. But they are only a part; they are not the total yajna, nor do they represent the totality of the meaning of yajna. The real meaning of yajna is generation, production, distribution, propagation and culmination. This applies to each and every situation in life. Therefore, it is very important to maintain the discipline of the yajna.

Yajnas are performed everywhere in the world and in different ways. But the yajna in which you are participating here is a yajna in the real sense, as Sri Swamiji has explained, because in a yajna to have real experience three constituents – production, distribution and conclusion – must be observed. In the *Bhagavad Gita*, yajnas of different types are mentioned. Just pouring ghee on the fire, making oblations and chanting mantras does not constitute a yajna. These components can be part of a yajna because mantras definitely have a sacred place in the yajna. Invocation of the shakti symbolically through appropriate mantras has an important place. The other important part of the yajna is *daan*, offering. Offering does not only denote giving. If you take something out of your pocket and hand it over to someone, that cannot truly be an offering. The feeling of offering all that you have, including your life, is really an offering in the truest sense.

20

Discipline of the yajna

The discipline of the yajna had already been explained. You have come with that aim in mind because you have come to participate in the yajna with a feeling of trust and devotion. You have come here to be in the holy presence of Sri Swamiji, not for entertainment. Hence it is of paramount importance that everyone is on time for the yajna. Be disciplined and behave in accordance with the rules of the yajna. Do not spoil this rare opportunity by going out for tea or a smoke or the like. Some of you may have the habit of devouring food during the session. Such habits do not allow you to maintain the concentration and discipline that is a must for such a sacred and pious occasion. Only after the necessary concentration and devotion have been inculcated through some sort of discipline involving your body and mind will you be able to secure what you have come for. If you desire to obtain the grace of this yajna by doing what you are accustomed to doing normally, then you are deceiving yourself.

Discipline is a part of the Indian tradition and this yajna is being performed as a continuation of that true and uninterrupted tradition. You must also be aware that yajna is performed in the whole being of a human being, not just in the *yajnashala*, the place where the yajna is conducted. In a yajna like this, there is a communion of physical, external, internal and subtle thoughts and actions.

So, you must come fully prepared to be a part and parcel of this yajna. If you feel cold, you should bring warm clothes. You must control your physical and mental habits. Such control is needed during the whole period of the yajna which begins on the fifteenth of December and concludes on the nineteenth. We all have to train ourselves for that auspicious occasion. As Sri Swamiji often says, "Why did the horse stop? Why did the betel nut deteriorate? Why did the disciple go astray?" Because they were not properly trained. It is only after proper training that strength is obtained. This strength comes only when there is conflict. You cannot have it if you sit idle. You cannot find this strength just by sitting in a meditative pose. It is for this reason that the *Gita* and

21

other scriptures speak of karma, not just meditation. So remember this and come prepared to participate in to-morrow's program.

Practical gifts

Sri Swamiji: Many participants have asked about the type of gifts they should bring. Whatever you give should be practical, something that is useful, not to rich people but to poor people. What does a poor man need? He doesn't need a candle, he needs a lantern. He doesn't need a little idol of Ganesha, he needs a bottle of kerosene oil. The gifts of the yajna have to be practical because they are given to the poor people around us who don't have much. When people give very fancy gifts, I tell them that I will have to give them to those who have a lot of money. If rich people come I give them a walkie-talkie. What will these poor people do with a walkie-talkie? I give walkie-talkies to rich people who come from Deoghar or Pune. Some of you will be getting one; they are of no use here.

In yajna the significance of a gift is that it is for the ordinary person. Rich people don't need a gift at all; they should be givers rather than receivers. Therefore, you have to ask me exactly what type of gift needs to be given. A gift is not just to please someone. A gift is not just to pass on your emotion to someone. Gifts should have some practical purpose, to help a person in need, whether it is a blanket, a pashmina shawl, a pair of shoes, an umbrella, a hurricane lantern, a satchel for a school child, a compass or a pencil case. I have lists of items to be given. Don't purchase anything else. Otherwise you will bring sweets like barfi and sandesh. A man doesn't live by barfi and sandesh. A poor man has certain definite needs in life, especially in this country. You know that very well and if you don't know, I'm just making it very clear to you. The people around you do not need the things you love. What is the use of a transistor or even a television set?

Gifts have to be offered pragmatically. A newborn baby requires nappies, which is also practical too as such useful things can be had cheaply. One of my disciples brought a microwave oven, which I declined because I do not need such things personally and these rural folk, whose welfare is supreme to me, cannot use it. So I did not accept it. In the same manner one disciple brought a gas oven. Now poor village folk can't use it as a gas cylinder for the oven would cost more than two hundred and fifty rupees. A poor man hardly gets forty rupees a day. Maybe for three months in a year he gets forty rupees a day, if at all. With that he has to have his daughter married and look after his medical bills. Therefore, please do not bring anything of your own choice, but find out from me what needs to be given. Don't do it for your own pleasure.

Live for the pleasure of others

One should live and do for the pleasure of others. You all know this, as you live for the well-being of your children. But at times people forget about it, which may be the outcome and influence of Western culture. Western culture, which has reached us like the unstoppable west wind, says to live for oneself. It is not wrong to live for your own well-being, but you should not forget the well-being of others. You should take care of their well-being along with your own.

You should also be aware that when you bring milk, sweets and fruit, I do not touch them. I only need a few rotis and a little dal once a day. I do not need anybody else's share. So I do not need to beg for bread for myself. I was also not born into the dynasty of those who generally beg, like the brahmins do. According to the four karmic divisions, *kshatriyas,* warriors, and *vaishyas,* merchants, do not beg, rather they offer to others. Those of you who are brahmins should not take it amiss, because you too would agree that the brahmin's main karma was to beg. This has been so from time immemorial. Our scriptures also speak about it. *Shudras,* labourers, also used to beg. But vaishyas and kshatriyas do not beg, rather they give. A kshatriya will not beg, but if necessary he will take what he desires by force. So when these sweetmeats come to me, I distribute them to others.

When you think about others, ponder these matters. Never act according to your own weaknesses and feelings. It is most important to know that two thirds of the total population lives in poverty, not only in India, but in other countries too. The poverty stricken outnumber the affluent. We cannot help all the poor, but at least we should all be aware of our duties to the downtrodden. This is a fact of life which you must all understand.

Share the responsibility

You should remember that more than two thirds of the human population is impoverished. They are having a very hard time in Africa, Southeast Asia and many other countries. I have been to their countries and lived with them. It is very important that the other one third of humanity shares the responsibility. If not, then the two thirds will increase and a time will come when the whole society will become insecure and the one third will be in danger. It is social science that I am talking about. Therefore, the two thirds of humanity must know that they have their well-wishers among us, that there are some people who think about them.

I'm not saying that we should pay for their education, although it would be good to do so, but at least they should have two square meals a day for their children. There are millions of families in this world whose children do not have two square meals a day. I am talking about children, not adults. If you have been following the plight of the children in Afghanistan recently, you will have seen with your own eyes that the same conditions are everywhere. They don't have anything to eat and the government is not able to look after them. I am not a critical man. I have never been in politics, nor do I wish to be. I'm not a critic in that way, but governments can't do anything. They are only busy constructing stadiums, very big things, whereas millions are just starving.

Atmabhava

We who have enough of everything should develop the philosophy of *atmabhava* in our lives. That is the philosophy

24

of Vedanta: you and I are the same. I often pray to God for another birth and an early departure, because at this advanced age I am not as effective in serving people as I would be if I had a new life. When I see these young people fully absorbed in their own selfish ends, I crave even more for a new life because I do not aspire for pleasure and riches, nor do I crave for a kingdom. My only craving is to serve those who are deprived and living in need. So, I pray to God to bless me with a new birth, in a poor family where one feels the pangs of hunger, where one undergoes the torture of cold without adequate clothing, and where one lives and dies in sickness without proper treatment. The pangs of the illiterate mother whose son takes birth and lives in poverty is difficult to fathom. So, I intend to have a life of hardship and rise from there.

My guru, Swami Sivananda, used to say that most sannyasins and sadhus are wasting their time in India because they are in pursuit of their own salvation. It is funny that when the majority of people are dying of hunger, these sadhus eat good food and pray for their salvation. What a surprise! When I asked my guru what to do, he said that he had already said what he had to say. Now I fully understand his vision. So, when this yajna is being performed, I pray only for the health and prosperity of everyone. Let everyone be kind and caring to one another and may no one ever experience any distress in their life.

Satsang 3

December 11, 2001

*I*f you are enjoying the music, God is also enjoying it and if you don't like it, perhaps He doesn't like it either. So be careful. When you sing, God sings too. I can say this with confidence; it is guaranteed. When you feel good, He feels good. When you do not feel good, He feels accordingly. So, if you want God to like what you do, you should do good things. If you sing a bhajan in praise of the Lord, you should sing it with full devotion. This is the basis of receiving God's grace.

Kirtan

The system of kirtan I have developed is the Satyananda system, the Munger system. It is unique; you will not find it anywhere else in India. Elsewhere in India there is no system to kirtan. People shout and don't listen to each other. Here we are aware of God's name. You will not get this exalted feeling anywhere else in India. The kirtan 'Govinda jaya jaya Gopala jaya jaya' being sung now will stop in ten minutes, as there are other important programs to follow. Otherwise if it were to continue for more than an hour, many of you would go into a trance, into *bhava samadhi*. That is certain. If you were to continue singing this kirtan with rapt devotion in the same rhythm, slowly and steadily, and climax very slowly, you would go into a trance. That is why I will stop it, because it is not the right time to go into bhava samadhi. Swami Sivananda used to say, "God's name is the quickest, safest, cheapest, surest and best way to reach God." He said 'safest'. Kundalini yoga is not the safest. Tantra is not the safest. No other way is sure except kirtan. Chanting of God's name with devotion is the national highway to reach Him.

George Harrison

There was a Western singer named George Harrison, a member of the Beatles group which created a tempest from 1964 to 1968. When Maharishi Mahesh Yogi and the Hare Krishna movement of A.C. Bhaktivedanta Swami Prabhu-pada began, these young people from the West, especially George Harrison and John Lennon, who were spearheading the Beatles' movement, came into contact with spiritual leaders. They were only in their early twenties then. Before George Harrison died recently, he said, "O God of love, I pray you shall live with me." Now in India, we all know that Krishna is the God of love. When we heard of George Harrison's departure, we were all saddened. His death was painful not only for devotees here, but for people around the world who knew him. His wife and son came to Triveni, the confluence of the Ganga, Saraswati and Yamuna at Prayag, and immersed his ashes there.

The Beatles visited the ashram of Sri Mahesh Yogi at Rishikesh in 1968. George Harrison was the forerunner of this generation who have now flooded the ashrams in India. There is hardly any ashram where you will not find Western-ers who have followed in the footsteps of George Harrison. They find solace in the ashrams of India. They do not get air conditioners or room heaters or knives and forks, yet they rest and pray in these ashrams so happily it is beyond the imagination. The happiness they find further proves how deeply influenced this generation was by George Harrison. The path of devotion is not an exclusively Indian way of life; it is the outpouring of the heart's feelings. And since every one of us has a heart, we know the secret of love and devotion.

To love God is not religion. To love God is not Hinduism or Christianity. Love is a personal feeling, a personal accomplishment, a personal necessity. Either you love the transitory life or you love the eternal life. Either you love Krishna or you love the world. When the emotions go to maya, to prakriti, to the fleeting things of the world, then it is an anti-climax. When the emotions that usually go to the worldly senses and towards maya turn to God, that is a climax. So today, in memory of George Harrison we will sing the kirtan 'Bhajo Radhe Krishna Gopala Krishna Krishna Krishna Sri Radhe'. This kirtan was very close to his heart.

When George Harrison breathed his last, he was fully conscious and he said, "O Lord, be with me always. When the soul leaves this body, may your name be on my lips. Let there be a tulsi plant, the Mother Ganga and the peepal tree before me when I die." This was the devotion of George Harrison. And why not? When a lover dies, he craves the presence of his beloved. This was the magnitude of his love for the Lord. He was so happy to see his Lord when his soul left his mortal body.

Love and sweetness

Lord Krishna was the incarnation of celestial love on earth, an element that is missing everywhere today. At present we have everything, but we lack love. Love is that aspect of emotion where you think about others, not about yourself. That is love. Love is giving, not taking and expecting. Love is sacrifice. Love is not an act. Love does not expect anything. If I love you, I do not expect anything from you. Love is just sacrifice. It is just giving, it is just dedicating, it is total consecration of your emotions. Sri Krishna was the symbol of that aspect of life.

> *Adharam madhuram badanam madhuram*
> *Nayanam madhuram hasitam madhuram*
> *Hridayam madhuram gamanam madhuranam*
> *Madhuradhipaterakhilam madhuram.*

28

When he walked, it was love that walked, when he smiled, it was love that smiled and when he laughed, it was love that laughed. *Madhuradipaterakhilam madhuram* – "O God! You are nothing but sweet love." Kirtan is nothing but love and sweetness. With this spirit we will sing with you.

Experiencing the lila

Tomorrow the lilas of Sri Krishna will be presented here for three days. In the past the gods and goddesses used to visit this earth surreptitiously to see the Lord's *lila*, divine pastimes, but now they come openly. The eternal bliss that you experience in the Lord's rasalila is indescribable. Just as you experience the nectar in halwa and rasgulla, in the same way there is an outcome of *rasa*, nectar, when we see the lila of the Lord.

The lilas to be enacted here will bestow on us the same sort of eternal bliss, *ananda*. They will have a special significance for the rural folk from Rikhia and the adjoining villages. Those of you from the West actually experience this type of lila in real life. Westerners have the feeling for rasalila as they have an understanding of dancing and singing, but people living in this backward area may not have those experiences, especially the children who have yet to see the world around them. Those of you who are now grown up and have become older will have to teach your children properly. Your train has already left and you have missed it. Now it is the young people's turn to catch this train which may take them to their desired destination. Therefore, you must bring them tomorrow so they can be a part of this lila.

Error of vision

What Tulsidas calls *drishtidosha*, defective vision, I call a cataract. This is the *ahamkara*, the ego, within all of us. We should pray to the Lord so that he knocks at our door and removes this cataract from our eyes. As you know, when you have cataracts in your eyes you cannot see what is in front of you. Even though the Lord is in front of us, we fail to see Him. This blind spot is truly man's ego. The funniest thing

29

is that you do not even know you suffer from this ego. You pray to Him to remove this ego, but you are not aware of the concept of ego. If I were to say that you are egoistic, you would retort, "Oh no, it is not so." You would claim to be a very good person.

So, the first point is that many of us do not see our ego. It is like defecating but refusing to look at our faeces because we regard it as dirty. We flush it away or call the sweeper to pick it up and throw it away. No one has seen this ego. What is its shape? Our scriptures and the Vedantic texts have described this ego in detail, but still no one tries to visualize it. No one feels for it and so no one understands it. That is why we pray to the Lord to keep us clean of this dirty word ego. We pray, "Take this self away from me, I can't use it anymore." Although Morarji Desai, our former Prime Minister, drank his urine, no one eats their faeces except, of course, the Aghoris who do not differentiate between anything found in this creation. The rest of us do not need it at all. So we say, "I can't use it anymore."

The whole world is in deep crisis because of this self or ego. Kingdoms are breaking down. Homes are falling apart. Even couples who have sworn to love each other quarrel publicly because of that very powerful ego. Our seers have declared that this feeling of self is a personality aberration. It is the greatest obstacle between God and the devotee. So, whatever you may say, I do not know why people are so egoistic. I also do not know why I feel the presence of God but do not experience His presence all the time. What happens during these experiences I also fail to recollect. Why this is so, I am unable to explain. Maybe it happens because of my self. The day that this self is completely obliterated then, like a pitcher full of water breaking in the sea, my own self will merge with the Almighty. Then neither you nor your ego are there, both are lost and merge together.

Power of music and dance

This is the era of music, song and dance. In every house and street you can hear music tapes being played because people enjoy it. It is absolutely necessary. If you go into bhava samadhi after singing a kirtan, you should not be surprised; it happens as a result of chanting God's name. I have had this experience in many of the musical conferences in and outside this country. In the Western world, where people generally do not have spiritual feelings, where boys and girls sing just for pleasure and entertainment, they also lose their self-awareness. They become so emotional and crazy about the music that they forget their self-identity. Music and kirtan is so powerful that it can free the purusha from prakriti; it can free the *jiva,* the individual soul, from the bondage of maya. So I say, "Do not hold back while singing."

Music has a great power which man has discounted. We should make use of it. Through kirtan you can reach the highest pinnacle of spiritual experience. Not by yoga or by any other means, but by kirtan alone you can have the vision of the Divine. You can have the vision of your Self. You can have the vision of God. You can have the vision of Christ. You can have the vision of Mary. You can have the vision of Krishna. You can have the vision of Rama. It is possible. Music does the most important groundwork by taking your self away from you. Music has so much inherent power that it can free you of your ego. The element of ahamkara would be totally eliminated if you were to follow the above prescription.

In my childhood I had these experiences in my birthplace, Kumaon, where the famous dancer Uday Shankar had his Cultural Centre. When I was about ten years old I started learning dancing at his centre. Uday Shankar and I performed together right up to 1962. During that period, when I practised I would lose contact with time, place, object and environment. I would forget everything connected with my own body and mind. All I would remember was the rhythm and timing of the dance sequence. This is the power of music and dance.

Lord Krishna was a great dancer. He used to dance with the gopis and the cowherders and those dance sequences are now depicted in the *Srimad Bhagavatam* as rasalila. Krishna's dance with the gopis on full moon night shows explicitly that through such devotional dance and song one can experience the presence of the Lord and become completely lost in devotion to Him.

Some of you practise hatha yoga because you suffer from diabetes, obesity or other illnesses. Hatha yoga can help to reduce your fat, it can help you in many ways, but it certainly can't remove your ignorance. The yoga that removes ignorance is bhakti yoga. I am not demeaning hatha yoga; it cleans your bowels and strengthens and purifies your nerves. But to progress on the spiritual path and to go deeper, you will have to undertake the path of bhakti. I have explained to you the way of devotion through kirtan. Besides this you will have to contemplate, especially to proceed further on this path. The most important part is whether you experience God's presence during this devotion. How do you define your relationship with God? These are just some of the issues you will have to think about.

Sincerity of purpose

I am sending swamis out to see who is loitering. So far I haven't received any reports from anyone and I hope I won't because we have to be very sincere to the purpose, not serious but sincere. The purpose is certainly spiritual. We have come here to gain, not to lose. If we have to lose anything, we have to lose bad habits, not good ones. So during the program, during kirtan, during pooja, it is best to stay seated for the length of the program, whether it is one hour or four hours. There will be four days preparation from the fifteenth to the eighteenth of December and the final pooja will be on the nineteenth. During these four days you will have to prepare yourself and make adjustments so that you can manage your prostate gland. At my age I should also have prostate gland problems, but I have had to prepare myself, because during the yajna I must be here. I can't go out for this and that. I have to find a way by which I will be able to sit here for one to four hours without any difficulty.

32

During that period mantras will be chanted, rituals will be performed and I have to imbibe, I have to inhale the atmosphere that will be generated. Remember that these are moments of experience. These experiences do not come for a long period of time, they come just as a glimpse. Maybe at that time, when the environment and atmosphere is ready, you are somewhere else. Don't miss it. Because just as the mantras, the yajna, the congregation of hundreds of people will be generating a divine environment, a divine energy, a divine atmosphere, all your spiritual aspirations, the totality of your sincerity, the totality of your positive intentions, will also be generating something here. If you generate bad thoughts you will receive them back. If you generate pure thoughts, a pure atmosphere, you will receive that. That is the law of nature.

So during the period of the yajna just forget everything else for the time being. Although you can do without kirtan until tomorrow, still you just remember kirtan. You can't remember God, someone has to remind you to remember God, but you remember your cigarettes. These are some of the issues that are very much linked with our life. The linkages have to be snapped for the time being as long as you are here. When you return home, you can do as you like because I won't be there and my CIA agents won't be there.

When you have come so far away from home, travelled such a long distance and spent so much money, you must have some purpose. Such a purpose must be good and pious. It is clear that you have not come here to loiter or to chatter or to create trouble. You are definitely here because of some virtuous and useful thoughts. There are no two opinions about it. We do not doubt your intentions. Surely all of you are here to participate in this yajna and obtain the benefits of this participation. Your motto must be to be blessed with the prasad, the grace, of the divine. We call this divine grace *kripa*, but in Christianity they use the words God's grace. The Lord will bestow the same grace upon you here and that is your purpose in coming.

Catching a glimpse of the divine

You have come here to obtain divine grace. Whatever your concept of God is, no one can challenge it because your concept of God is God. Whatever you think about God is correct, but some of us do pick up bad habits. Once a blind man enquired about the location of the castle gate. He was told that if he walked alongside the wall touching it with his hand, he would find the gate by himself. But just when the gate was near, from habit the blind man started scratching his body and thus passed the gate without realizing it was there.

Once the yajna starts and the mantra chanting begins and the process of invoking the gods and goddesses takes shape, the whole atmosphere becomes charged. A charged energy field is created which is reflected in a glimpse of the divine power. It can be visible momentarily only to those who are alert and careful. It happens so suddenly that it flashes like lightning, after sparkling for a few moments over this time and space. If you are outside fulfilling the demands of your old habits, there is every likelihood that you will miss having that rare glimpse and be deprived of that divine grace for which you came all this way. When the prasad, God's grace, came to this venue, you were not here to receive it.

You can smoke when you go back to your hotels. You can live in a hotel, you can have a bottle, you can go total, I don't mind. Hotel, bottle, total, that is your destiny. But I'm talking about the yajna from the fifteenth to the nineteenth of December. So gird up your loins. This is not a very hard task. Everyone should discipline themselves. Discipline is the means, not the end. What is the outcome of discipline? You receive the grace, the prasad, of God. This year the invocation of Devi will begin on the fifteenth. The yajna will be established that morning. Then you will all receive the grace of the divine with the seal of the Mother Goddess. Devi's prasad will come to you with Her authentication. If you are loitering outside the venue, you will not receive it. That is very clear as it is His commandment to me.

Prasad – symbol of God's grace

I want to tell you one very important thing. God tells me what to do. I don't ask God for anything, although I don't mind asking, because if I feel shy about asking from God, I am a foolish man. If you miss this opportunity once, you will have to beg God yourself, which you can do once or one hundred times. I do not need anything for myself so I will not beg for you. That much is certain.

God gives to me and tells me what to do. He has told me that this year I will have to give a token of prasad, a token of grace. It may be a *tabiz*, an amulet, which will be symbolic of God's grace. If I offer you a pashmina shawl, do not feel that it is from me. Swami Satyananda does not have that capacity because everything in the world is His property. So if you receive a pashmina shawl from me, then you should know that you have received a symbol of God's grace although it has come to you through me. It is not an offering or a selfless act or righteousness on my part. It is only God's grace, which you may get in any form. You are, however, at liberty to beg from God directly. There is no objection to that, but my duty is to give this prasad to you.

When your name is announced, you must be here to receive the prasad. If you are absent and then demand the prasad later on, it will not be available. It will lapse like the government's allotment, which lapses if not drawn at the proper time. God's grace can lapse too! If you are not here when your name is called you will miss out this year. You may say, "But my name was there." Yes, your name was there, but it has been cancelled. The laws of the Almighty are quite different. Once a saint told me that God visits your abode many times. I said, "Yes, that is true, but how would I recognize Him?" He replied, "Never expect God to present Himself before you in his four-handed form, as He did not show this form to Arjuna without being begged first." Arjuna had to pray for it.

God's grace comes to us in many forms, but why are we deprived of receiving that grace? Because we fail to grab such a rare opportunity in all earnestness. A farmer grows crops by

35

sowing the seeds at the right time. If he fails to do that even for a day or two, then the crop will definitely fail. Just as the cultivation is done after visualizing the right moment, just as a marriage is performed according to the right congregation of stars, so God's grace can be had in the same fashion by strictly observing certain rules and procedures.

Satsang 4

December 12, 2001

Sri Swamiji: (singing in praise of Lord Rama) O God, I beg you again and again to bestow your blessings on me. My prayer is simple. I am asking for a boon. Please grant me that boon gladly so that I may have unwavering concentration, love and devotion for your lotus feet at all times. May your satsang always be a part of my life. These are the twin boons that will help us throughout our life, in joy as well as in sorrow.

Sri Krishna – a natural life

Swami Niranjan: Today we will witness an enactment of the lilas of Sri Krishna by the Rasalila Institute of Vrindavan. Rasalila is a most important concept to Indians. Krishna was not a very gentle child. He used to steal butter, tease the girls, beat the boys and do all the not so nice things that a child likes to do. Once, when I was a small boy, I went to a Christian convent. The nuns said to me, "Don't do this. Don't do that." When I asked, "What should I do?" they said, "Do as I wish!" Now should a child of eight behave like a woman of thirty-five? If a small child had been present, he would have told me to jump up and down, give a slap and spit in his eye!

Sri Swamiji: A child cannot teach another child! Sri Krishna was an incarnation of God, not an ordinary child. He had to take birth to give lessons to the children. Sri Krishna led a very natural life like a child should lead – to be a good child, a great child, a powerful child, to be a philosopher, to be God, to be a friend, to be a warrior. At the same time he loved all the girls of his time. If he had been born now you would all be very happy! The gopis did not marry because Krishna loved them all. If there was one man who could love all of you, why would you marry at all?

If you go deep into Sri Krishna's life, you will find a new social thought, a new religious thought and a new philosophical thought, which we do not find in Semitic civilizations. Educated people in this country are not graduates of Vedic thought. You have not been taught Vedic philosophy and culture. The way you think and behave, the morality you practise, the do's and don'ts you follow are not part of the Vedic lifestyle. You follow the path shown by foreign cultures. What you practise now is the result of three or four hundred years of compulsory education along these lines.

You can learn from Lord Krishna's rasalila how a child should be born, how he should be nurtured and cared for. You will see this in the splendid rasalila to be performed here shortly. Where there is tolerance, everything is okay. What I see is my God. My God is in me. My God is my personal God. We are all polytheists here – a few days for Rama; Krishna today, tomorrow and the day after; Devi, the mother, from the fifteenth to the nineteenth; Christ on December the twenty-fifth; then New Year's day for myself!

Avatar of love

Swami Niranjan: Krishna has many followers throughout the world. The ISKCON movement has propagated the glory, history and life of Sri Krishna. The world has never seen a person like Sri Krishna. He was a playboy, a philosopher, an orator, a yogi, a fighter, a saint. All the qualities you can think of are contained in him. He is also the indweller of all hearts, especially in this modern age, because he is the epitome of beauty, grace, love and dynamism.

38

Prior to Krishna's birth, atrocities were being committed in the world. When the people prayed for relief from the suffering, their prayers were heard. Sri Swamiji has mentioned that God comes down when we call Him. When prayers from the heart reach God, then God manifests in a human form. The events which led to Krishna's birth will be enacted today, including his early childhood, how he destroyed the demons, the terrorists, and how he lived his life in a playful way, sometimes stealing butter, sometimes duping people, sometimes teasing, sometimes dancing with the gopis and becoming their heartthrob.

This enactment is being presented by artists from Vrindavan Rasalila Sansthan, led by Swami Hara Govinda Maharaj. It is a very famous group, one of the best in India. They are all devotees of Sri Radhe. You should know that there is only one man in the world here and that every other person in this creation is female. You may not understand this, because you may look at your body and say, "But I'm a man and she's a woman."

Sri Swamiji: Christians understand this concept. In Christianity there is the concept of being married to Christ.

Swami Niranjan: Whether you believe it or not, *bhaktas*, devotees of the Lord, know that in front of the Lord we are all females. Even when Lord Shiva went to have darshan of Sri Krishna, he had to dress like a woman. He had to get rid of his snakes and wear jewellery. He had to get rid of his bhasma and tiger skin and wear a *lehnga-choli*, a skirt and blouse, lipstick and eye shadow. Krishna definitely symbolizes the epitome of love. He is the avatar of love and it is that love which we lack in our lives today. So, experience the love which flows through Sri Krishna.

Sri Swamiji: Sri Krishna has brought life to philosophy and religion, otherwise they are so abstract that you always have to wear a castor oil face or a Sunday face. He has brought life to religion and philosophy so that we can also smile while we are in church. There is only one culture and civilization in this world where the gods dance, sing and play with the gopis, where they playfully steal and participate in wars and at the same time give enlightenment. Where will you find such a civilization, except in India!

Swami Niranjan: Lord Krishna is the symbol of God with all His attributes and you will have the opportunity to witness His lilas today.

Lesson of the Gita

Sri Swamiji: There is a song in which it has been sung that Lord Krishna who was the charioteer of Arjuna in the *Mahabharata* was actually known as Rama in the Treta age. If there had been no Lord Krishna, there would have been no *Srimad Bhagavad Gita*. The *Gita* is like the cream in milk. It is the synthesis of all the shastras. Among all the Vedas, among all the religions of the world, the *Gita* is the cream of them all. In the *Gita Dhyanam* it is said,

Sarvopanishado gaavo dogdhaa Gopaalanandanah
Paartho vatsah sudhir bhoktaa dugdham Gitaamritam mahat.

"All the Upanishads are the cows, the milker is Krishna, the cowherd boy Partha (Arjuna) is the calf, people of purified intellect, the listeners to and readers of the Gita, are the drinkers, the milk is the great nectar of the Gita."

Where did the Lord give this lesson? He did not give it in a temple, or a mosque or a church or an ashram. He gave it on the battlefield where men were preparing to fight with each other. Such knowledge is useful in a conflict in the same way as you need medicine when you are sick. Why? Because during these conflicts people are in distress, they get hurt, they lose their kith and kin. It is on the battlefield that people are wounded and die and so this nectar of knowledge, the *Gita*, came out of the Lord's mouth to provide relief.

In the *Gita* the Lord said only one thing: do your duty – that is your dharma. Do not be concerned about the result of your actions. You will reap the fruits of the karmas of your past births. You will get the fruits of this birth maybe in the next birth. This is what Lord Krishna told Arjuna. Lord Krishna was unique in the sense that he was the only one in

40

the world who could impart this message when a great battle was imminent.

God has many forms

Sri Krishna was a perfect man, a *poorna purusha*. The West needs no introduction to Sri Krishna. Westerners are searching for yoga in bhoga; they are not searching for bhoga in yoga. They are searching for perfection in this imperfect world. Sri Krishna said that in this trifling world, in this world of struggle, we have to find peace. So Westerners need no introduction to Sri Krishna, only a reminder.

Frankly speaking, we believe that God is everything. We give a few days to Sri Rama, a few days to Sri Krishna, a few days to Devi, a few days to Christ; we are all polytheists. We do not believe in a set definition of God. To give a set definition of God is monotheism and the effect of monotheism in the long run can be felt in society, civilization and politics, as well as in parliament. That is why, although it is said, "There is only one Brahman; there was none else except Him," still we believe in Rama, Krishna, Devi, Durga, Hanuman and so on. To say that God is only this and nothing else is an intolerant definition of God. Have you seen God? How then could you say that God is only this? You have not seen Him and therefore He may be like this, may be like this, may be like this, *neti, neti, neti*.

Polytheism is not merely philosophy, it is a source of politics, a source of man's behaviour, a source of civilization. Where has terrorism originated? When you have a set definition of religion, a set definition of God and a set definition of your culture and civilization, then you are on the way to destruction. Therefore, Sri Krishna said, "In whichever form you remember the Lord, you will see Him in that form." You see God in whichever form you pray to Him. God does not have one form, God has many forms. The Lord is in the sun, the moon, the sky, the earth, in water, on earth, on all sides, in the mountains, in fire, in the whole universe. Every shape and form is the Lord. He is Vishnu, who is everywhere. You can see God in any form.

41

Krishna lila

Swami Niranjan: The rasalila will now begin. The mangal-acharan, the invocation, and the arati are from *Hanuman Chalisa*.

Sri Swamiji: The story being rendered here is as told in the tenth chapter of the *Srimad Bhagavatam* published by ISKCON, the International Society for Krishna Consciousness. Kamsa, the demonic king, had given his sister, Devaki, in marriage to the prince Vasudeva. While he was taking the bride and bridegroom home in their chariot there was a divine mandate, a divine voice, that announced, "Kamsa, the eighth child of this sister will kill you." Kamsa immediately decided to kill his own sister. Eventually, however, he agreed to let her live. Kamsa imprisoned Vasudeva and Devaki in Mathura. Each year for six years Devaki gave birth to a male child and Kamsa destroyed them all as he was afraid that any one of them might be Krishna.

Commentator: When Devaki was expecting the seventh child the Lord ordered the appearance of his Yogamaya in the land of Vraj, in Vrindavan. Here Rohini, the elder wife of Vasudeva, was residing with Nanda and his wife Yashoda. Nanda was the chief of Gokul, the loveliest village in Vraj. The Lord directed Yogamaya to transfer the seventh foetus from Devaki's womb to Rohini's. The seventh child was Balarama, the elder brother of Krishna. Even today, Baladeva Chhath, in memory of Balarama's birth is celebrated in Vraj, but at that time it was celebrated secretly for fear of Kamsa. Meanwhile Vasudeva informed his captor's guards that the seventh conception had aborted. The servants and guards ran to their king, Kamsa, and raised slogans of his glory – "Victory to our king, the seventh pregnancy has aborted."

Birth of Krishna

Swami Niranjan: When the eighth child, Krishna, was born to Devaki and Vasudeva, he appeared to them as the Lord and ordered Vasudeva to take him to Gokul and replace him with the daughter who had just been born to Nanda and Yashoda. This daughter was Yogamaya. Vasudeva immediately escaped from Mathura and took Krishna to Gokul.

As soon as Kamsa, the terrorist, found out that the eighth child had been born, he went to the prison and found that it was a girl. When Kamsa tried to kill her she appeared as the eight-armed Durga and said, "How can you kill me? The child who will kill you has already been born somewhere within this world. Nothing can save you now." Overwhelmed with fear, Kamsa began to plan the death and destruction of Krishna and arranged for all the children born within the last ten days to be killed.

Commentator: Meanwhile in Gokul Nanda joyfully celebrated the birth ceremony of Krishna. When the cowherd men and women of Vraj learnt that Nanda and Yashoda had had a son they were overwhelmed with joy. They dressed themselves in costly garments and ornaments as if for a festival and engaged in jubilant celebrations. The gopis applied kumkum to their foreheads and ran to Nanda's house, singing these songs:

> *Happiness to Nanda*
> *Victory to Kanhaiya Lal, Victory to Kanhaiya Lal.*
>
> *The women of Vraj sparkle like 'barfi',*
> *The gopis and cowherders are singing a song*
> *As sweet as 'gujhiya',*
> *The lovely Baladeva is like 'peda'*
> *And his mother Rohini,*
> *Who is as beautiful as a juicy mango,*
> *Is like 'rasa kheer'.*

Kheer has become the rasa. It is all sweetened. Let there be some salty things too.

> *Nanda is king and he is salty,*
> *The village of Gokul is 'garam masala',*
> *Shyam is a 'jalebi'*
> *And Yashoda has produced a son like a 'laddoo'*
> *In a night which resembles 'rabadi'.*
> *Yes, in a night like 'rabadi'*
> *She has produced a son like a 'laddoo'.*

43

Swami Niranjan: Kamsa instructed the demoness Pootana to destroy all the babies born that month. Pootana, the terrorist chief, went to Gokul to kill Krishna. She took the form of Miss Universe and dressed like a beautiful woman entered the house of Yashoda, where she was destroyed by Krishna.

You have to remember that Gokul was a village of simple cowherd boys and girls, who did nothing but tend the cows, sell the milk and live a happy and simple life very much like the neighbours of Sri Swamiji in this area. They were very innocent people and Krishna lived among them, played with them and flirted with them. The early childhood of Krishna took place in Vraj.

As a child Krishna ate the butter and curd of the house and when his mother admonished him and told him that thieving was not appropriate for the son of the leader of the cowherders, Krishna told his mother that he would not stop thieving, that she could do anything she liked but that was something he would not stop. While the gopis of Vraj were preparing the yoghurt, butter and other items from milk, they sang kirtan and wished that Krishna would come to their homes to eat the yoghurt, to drink the milk and to be jolly with all his friends.

Sri Swamiji: Rasalila is a part of consciousness. Tomorrow we will see more of the rasalila. The Lord has stolen butter today. He will steal hearts tomorrow. He is the king of thieves. I bow to the Lord of thieves.

> *Let us perform arati of child Krishna.*
> *Let us sacrifice our body, mind and wealth to Him.*
> *He is the most loved one of Yashoda.*
> *He is the star in the eyes of Baba.*
> *He is the most loved one of the gopis.*
> *Let everyone sacrifice their life to Him.*
> *Let us perform arati of child Krishna.*

Swami Niranjan: Please remember that no one should try to touch Sri Swamiji's feet. The best method of salutation is to fold both your hands near your heart region and pay your respects to Sri Swamiji in that way.

Sri Swamiji: Many people come for a day or two and then suddenly leave without letting us know. Make a point of speaking to Swami Niranjan or Swami Satsangi before you go. Since the Devi worship has not yet started, you cannot receive Her prasad, but if you have to leave you will certainly receive the prasad of this akhara. Everyone will get that whether they are from Rikhia, elsewhere in India, from America, Germany, Russia or Afghanistan for that matter!

Satsang 5

December 13, 2001

Swami Niranjan: Lord Sri Rama and Lord Sri Krishna are the two most prominent and outstanding figures in Indian culture. They are remembered not because they are avatars of divinity, but because of the lives they lived which have become examples for everyone to emulate. The Indian mind is permeated with that entire concept – the laughter, games, wisdom and personalities of Sri Krishna and Sri Rama. In yesterday's drama Krishna was asked, "Why have you come down to this earth?" He replied, "Because here I will find abuse and suffering. In heaven nobody abuses me and there is no suffering. In my dimension there is nothing except peace and bliss. But here on earth I find people who can abuse me, people who can love me, people who can adore me, people who can reject me. It is here that I find suffering coexisting with pleasure." Therefore, Indian thought has always seen God existing everywhere, whether it is in peace, *shanti*, or the absence of peace, *ashanti*, whether it is in pleasure, contentment and happiness or in suffering.

Rasalila Institute

On behalf of all those who have arrived here on the occasion of Sita Kalyanam and Sat Chandi Maha Yajna, I welcome Sri Swami Hara Govinda Maharaj from the Rasalila Sansthan,

Vrindavan. Swami Hara Govinda Maharaj has dedicated his whole life to describing and exhibiting the lilas of Lord Krishna. He has received many awards for his work and has been awarded one of the highest honours by the Government of India. We are fortunate to have his gracious presence amongst us.

God is a reality

Sri Swamiji: There will be another rasalila recital today. I am reminding you again that we are polytheistic. We believe in one God – but an infinite God. One is not a mathematical one, it is a total one, *poornamidah poornamidam,* infinity as they say in modern physics. Our God is infinite, abstract. For thousands of years we have found that God should be seen as a reality. If you love your child, he is your God. If you love your girl friend, for you she is Radha.

Yesterday's depiction was of a man who lived as a man but who was a superman, a perfect man, a *poorna purusha*. He incarnated many thousands of years ago at the end of the cycle of Dwapara Yuga in order to destroy evil and restore righteousness. His name was Krishna. Although he was born into a royal family, his actual birth took place in a prison in Mathura. As a newborn he was smuggled to Gokul where he lived incognito for many years.

The story is told in the tenth chapter of the *Srimad Bhagavatam,* published by the Bhaktivedanta Book Trust. It is also told in the *Krishnavatar* series, published by K.M. Munshi of Bharatiya Vidya Bhavan. There Lord Krishna is a child but he is full of divinity. The story is told with sweetness, with melody, in a way that we can understand. It is one of the best stories about God. God must become the subject matter of stories! God must become the subject matter of music! God must become the subject matter of dance! God must become the subject matter of discussion and dialogue! God is not beyond dialogue. God is not beyond the mind. God is just here.

You should have a relationship with God in a way that you can understand Him, just as you understand your son, your father, your brother or anyone else. God should be understood first. If you start with a hypothesis that God is *ajneya*, unknowable, it's a problem. God is knowable, like x=5. Don't you find hypotheses in algebra where the value of x is known or has already been decided? Once you are told that God cannot be realized, then you think that is final. Close your books and start from where you can feel Him, like the love you give to your child. After all, love is God. You love your child, don't you? What are you expressing there? When you have a baby, what is your relationship with that baby? You are expressing God – love is God. So, that love which you are expressing for your child is a glimpse of God. Go ahead with x=5. You will find the ultimate answer at the end of that little sum. We say that the love for your child is the love of a glimpse of God.

Clapping – medicine for the heart

Clapping during kirtan is not for entertainment. Clapping is a cardiac exercise; it balloons the veins in the heart, which become contracted when one sings. The purpose of clapping is to relax the veins and assist the normal circulation of the blood to the heart. It not only heats the system and energizes the body, but at the same time it works on the heart. When the arteries become constricted the blood circulation stops, which causes a heart attack. In such a situation, physicians administer certain medicines which allow the blood to circulate again. So, clapping while singing kirtan or bhajans is just like medicine for the heart. Clapping is essential for spiritual life.

Now, if you feel that you are an important person and what would people say if you were to start clapping, then in that case you will have to pretend. But you should realize the importance of clapping. In olden times, girls from good families did not dance as people would criticize them, but now when they dance they are appreciated. This change has taken place. In the past, if a collector or commissioner started clapping, it was not appreciated, but now people say, "What a great devotee he is!" Isn't that a positive change? Laugh if it makes you feel lighter! At times joking is quite necessary to break the monotony. So whenever an occasion for clapping comes don't hesitate to do it. People should not hesitate to do two things – one is clapping and the other is laughing. One should not even suppress tears. You must know that tears, laughter, clapping and shouting are good for the health. Crying, clapping, laughing and dancing are part of bhakti yoga.

Dance of purusha and prakriti

Yesterday's rasalila presentation depicted the childhood of Sri Krishna, so it was called Krishna lila. Now Krishna has grown into a wild young lad, so it will be known as Gopi lila. The gopis are the cowherd girls. Finally it will culminate in maharasa, the great cosmic dance. Maharasa is one purusha and all of prakriti dancing. Purusha is in the centre and prakriti is all around him. In the Indian tradition purusha and prakriti is the concept of Samkhya philosophy. The *Bhagavad Gita* (13:19) states,

Prakritim purusham chaiva viddhyaanaadi ubhaavapi
Vikaaraamshcha gunaamshchaiva viddhi prakritisambhavaan.

"Know both prakriti and purusha as beginningless or eternal. Know also that all the modifications and qualities are born of prakriti."

Prakriti and purusha are the two factors behind the entire cosmos; creation, sustenance and dissolution, *pralaya*. Both are eternal, *anadi*; purusha is eternal and prakriti is eternal. Once prakriti and purusha dance together then life springs into action and there is the spring of life. That is so in physical life, in spiritual life, in mental life and also in the psychological arena of life. There has to be an association, a coming together of the two diametrically opposed forces. Prakriti is subject to change, *vikara*, and purusha is not subject to change. Prakriti is *parinami*, evolving, transforming; purusha is not.

That is the concept of maharasa according to the *Srimad Bhagavatam* and even according to physics. Those of you

49

who have studied physics will know about unified field theory. Maharasa is unified field theory depicted in Hindu mythology. Krishna represents purusha, the gopis represent prakriti. *Go* means senses. It is said in the *Ramacharitamanas*, *Go gochar jahan lagi man jai* – "When the self becomes involved with the senses, the goal of realizing the ultimate becomes obscured." The senses and purusha, prakriti and purusha. In unified field theory all the elements of nature are centred at one point of the universe. Everything is here. That is the concept of maharasa. Maharasa is the cosmic dance of purusha and prakriti, which was in the past, which is in this age and which will continue in the future. It is eternal. This cosmic dance is a replica of the dance of Krishna and the gopis. Radha is the agreeable power of the Lord. Although she is a woman, still she is not so. She is the cosmic power. Purusha and prakriti are one and many too. It cannot be explained.

Maharasa is the dance of boys and girls. When Michael Jackson dances that is also maharasa. When you see Bharata Natyam that is maharasa. You people also dance. People throughout the world dance from the time they are born. That is why one is compelled to say, "Oh Gopal! I have danced too much! Now I am tired." Here too in the akhara where I had come to rest, I am witnessing the dance.

In the *Bhagavad Gita* (7:4–5) this particular scene has been very aptly described by Sri Krishna.

Bhoomiraaponalo vaayuh kham mano buddhireva cha
Ahamkaara iteeyam me bhinnaa prakritirashtadhaa.
Apareyamitastvanyaam prakritim viddhi me paraam
Jeevabhootaam mahaabaaho yayedam dhaaryate jagat.

"Earth, water, fire, air, ether, mind, intellect and also ego – thus is my nature (prakriti) divided eightfold. This is the lower prakriti; know it as different from my higher prakriti, the life principle by which this world is upheld."

Here Sri Krishna has said that earth, water, fire, air, ether, mind, intellect and ego are his eightfold companions, prakritis of mind. These eight prakritis are the lower forms of nature, the manifest nature. Besides these eight prakritis there is one more – *para prakriti*, which is Radha. There is an unmanifest nature, *param buddhi*, beyond intellect. She is my transcendental companion and she represents Radha. Radha is para prakriti! The *sakhis* or companions are the eightfold lower prakriti and Krishna is the purusha who is the root of everything that exists.

Maharasa – cosmic dance

Once Kamadeva, whom you call Cupid, decided to do combat with Sri Krishna. He went to Sri Krishna and said that he wanted to do combat with him. Krishna said that there were two forms of combat: "In the first one I will sit in meditation, withdraw my senses and then you will order passion to strike me. If I am moved, I am defeated. If my mind does not move, if it is steady at the centre, then you are defeated. Passion, *kama,* is defeated. This is one form of combat. In the other form of combat I will dance with my girlfriends, my sakhis, and my gopis. If my mind is polluted, if my mind is corrupted by sensuality, then I am defeated. But if my mind remain unruffled and undisturbed then you are defeated."

"Which form of combat would you prefer?" Krishna asked Cupid. Cupid replied, "Well, the first one I have tried on Lord Shiva, I have tried it on many people. I would like to try the second one when you are dancing with your girl-friends. I want to see if your mind can be affected by sensuality, if your mind can be affected by the lower forces of maya." "Okay," said Krishna, "on Sharad Poornima, on the banks of the Yamuna I will be ready with the girls. Come!"

It is very difficult to explain the maharasa, but in modern Western terminology it is called cosmic dance. In this cosmic dance the principles of the entire universe come together. It is depicted here in the form of Krishna, Radha, Kamadeva, the seasons of summer, autumn, winter and spring; every possible element of nature, matter, is enshrined in this cosmic dance. This cosmic dance is so wide that from it you can interpret how the whole cosmos, the sun, the moon and the stars, manifested.

51

At the same time, the maharasa can also be understood in the form of yogic experience. This is very important, because when you talk about spirit and matter, purusha and prakriti, they are not necessarily physical, physiological or material; they are also in the spiritual field. That is why they talk about the purusha in sahasrara; the kundalini, the shakti, in mooladhara; the five elements: *akasha,* ether; *vayu,* air; *agni,* fire; *jala,* water; and *prithvi,* earth; the twin forces of the sun and moon, ida and pingala; and the seventy-two thousand nadis through which the kundalini goes in the whole process of elevation and awakening. That is also maharasa, what we call the cosmic play.

This cosmic experience has been explained in our Vedic system in many ways. In the *Bhagavad Gita* (11:3–4), Arjuna asks Krishna to reveal his *virat roopa,* his cosmic form.

Evametadyathaattha tvamaatmaanam parameshvara
Drashtumichchhaami te roopamaishvaram purushottama.
Manyase yadi tachchhakyam mayaa drashtumiti prabho
Yogeshvara tato me tvam darshayaatmaanamavyayam.

"O Lord, still I long to see your divine form. If you think it possible for me to see it, then, O Lord of the Yogis, reveal to me your imperishable form."

Then Krishna tells Arjuna (11:8),

Na tu maam shakyase drashtumanenaiva svachakshushaa
Divyam dadaami te chakshuh pashya me yogamaishvaram.

"As you are unable to behold me with your own eyes, I will give you divine eyesight. With this divine vision behold my divine power, the greatness of my existence, the existence of God."

Then Sri Krishna showed Arjuna his divine form.

So, the maharasa is not an ordinary event, but in the *Srimad Bhagavatam* it has been depicted very well. The dance of Radha and Krishna with the gopis is eternal, it is universal and it is ever present. Even while I am speaking, in every iota of this universe, this universe which is material, mental and spiritual – and maybe something else also – everything is dancing. Nuclear scientists say that atoms and molecules and electrons are dancing all the time. This dance of atoms is the bedrock of the entire creation. Speech, action, feeling, experience, creation and dissolution of each and every aspect of matter is nothing but a play. We have heard all that. But we are growing beyond the atom. The atom is one of the stages of matter, it is not ultimate matter. Although the literal meaning of the word atom is indivisible, the atom is divisible, it can be divided – *anu paramanu trisenu*.

Beyond matter there is mind, beyond mind there is self. In the *Bhagavad Gita* (3:42) Krishna says,

Indriyaani paraanyaahuh indriyebhyah param manah
Manasastu paraa buddhiryo buddheh paratastu sah.

"They say that the senses are superior to the body; superior to the senses is the mind; superior to the mind is the intellect; one who is superior even to the intellect is the self."

Beyond the indriyas is the mind, beyond the mind is buddhi, beyond buddhi is the self and beyond self there is the existence of something which has no form. Therefore, we are dealing with a very intricate subject; it is all a matter of personal experience.

Yogamaya

Something very important has been added here, which is Yogamaya. Krishna calls Yogamaya, his potency, and she says, "I'll serve you in any way." She provides a lot of services! The Lord's powers are Yogamaya and in this sense, if you analyze the philosophy of Adwaita Vedanta, then everything is just Yogamaya. Perhaps the Lord has created an illusion and we are talking and talking and nothing is really happening. You may even be dreaming, who knows? That is what Gaudapadacharya has said in *Gaudapada-Karika* (2:32),

Na nirodho na chotpathirna baddho na cha sadhakah
Na mumukshurna vai mukta ityesha paramarthata.

"Neither dissolution, nor again creation; neither bound, nor again aspiring for salvation; neither desirous of salvation, nor again emancipated – this is the highest truth."

53

That is absolutism. This is relative existence. You know about the theory of relativity. If you determine through the system of relativity, everything is related to time, space and object. But there is an absolute existence. What is the absolute existence? It is said that there is no creation at all, no dissolution, no doomsday. No one is bound. No one is a sadhaka. No one is a seeker of liberation. There is no moksha. This is the absolute definition of the entire creation. When I was a child of eight I used to wonder what was beyond the sun, what was beyond the moon. I couldn't understand it. Today I also wonder what the answer is. The only answer I get is that there can be no answer.

Duty to God

In the spiritual realm maharasa is the process of yoga where everything dissolves into one purusha, into one supreme self, one great spirit. The gopis have lost themselves and have become one with the form of Krishna. There is a very substantial dialogue between Sri Krishna and his sakhis, his girlfriends, the gopis. Purusha and prakriti have that relationship. Prakriti is my girlfriend! She is your girlfriend too. Sri Krishna played the flute; he is known as *bansidhara*, the flute bearer. When he played his flute, the gopis heard and they thought he was calling them. They went running after him in the middle of the night, on Sharad Poornima. Sri Krishna asked why they had come and he tried to discourage them in many ways. He told them to go home, over and again, that it was not right that they should come to him in the middle of the night because he was young and they were also young. But they were determined, they were adamant. They said, "No, you are our sole refuge. You are our centre and you are the goal of life."

Ultimately, they asked him a question, "Lord, did you not say to renounce everything and submit to you, to take shelter in you." "Yes," replied Krishna. "Then why are you telling us to go home?" asked the gopis. Krishna had no answer. Gradually, he submits to the demands of the gopis, and ultimately the rasalila takes place. Prakriti will come in

54

conjunction with purusha and there will be creation. There will be that spiritual experience that yoga calls nirvikalpa samadhi or Bhagavat darshan, whatever you call it.

God is the centre of life. Bhakti and love are the main duty of every human being. Animals only eat, sleep, procreate and seek security. Man alone can think of God. Man alone can investigate God. Man alone can dedicate his whole life to God. An elephant or a donkey or a snake or a peacock or a monkey can't do it. Only man can practise bhakti. If that is the truth and if that is the law of nature, then the prime duty of everyone is divine bhakti. Bhakti is the first duty. Family is the next duty.

This what the gopis told Krishna. Krishna tried to discourage them by saying, "Go home. Look after your children. Look after your husbands." But they said, "No, no, no! Those are secondary duties!" Vedic dharma also says the same thing. Even Christianity and Islam say the same thing. God first, everything else second if at all necessary. So, this is a most important dialogue.

Transcend duality

Now they are preparing for the maharasa. The news has spread everywhere. Lord Shiva has found out that Sri Krishna is going to have the great cosmic dance on the banks of the Yamuna, on Sharad Poornima, the full moon night in the month of Sharad. Shiva has come to Vrindavan to witness the dance. He encounters some of the gopis and tells them that he is going to witness that cosmic dance. "No, no, you can't do it," they say. When he asks why not, they reply, "As long as you are aware that you are a purusha, a male, you can't come. You have to transcend the idea of sex, the idea of this duality of nature." Shiva asked, "But how can I do it?" The gopis said, "Take a dip within *mansarovar*, the lake of the greater mind, and you will transcend that sexual duality. And then you can join our rasalila."

Therefore, when you have to enter into the depths of your consciousness, you definitely have to transcend the duality of nature with which you are intertwined all the time in your life. The real cosmic dance is when you are within yourself.

So, we will meet again tomorrow for the third day of this beautiful event when you can feel the presence of God in human beings and discuss how we can feel God in this body. Yes, we can feel Him bodily. We can feel His *nirakara* or formless attribute in a *sakara* form, His *nirguna* or formless form in a *saguna* form. The One will appear in various forms.

Satsang 6

December 14, 2001

The yajna will start tomorrow and the chanting of Ramacharitamanas Path will start at seven a.m. sharp followed by the invocation to the Mother Goddess. So you will have no leisure until noon. You will be here from seven to twelve and from two to six and you should not leave during that time. For four or five hours at a stretch, you will need to make yourself free from the botherations of going out to the toilet or for tea. So gird up your loins. These are important instructions, they are mandatory; they are not announcements or recommendations.

For those of you who want to participate in the yajna personally and psychologically, but cannot read *Durga Saptashati* in Sanskrit, I have printed a very simple mantra. It is *'Om Aim Hrim Klim Chamundaye Namah'*. It is a Navarna mantra. You can just keep repeating that mantra mentally, not with tense concentration, but with ease, as if you are reading a book, singing a song or watching television. I will give you a separate enclosure to sit in where you can do the japa. But remember that there should be no hypnotic meditation, no contemplation, no one-pointedness – just chanting. I'm not meditating now, I am talking to you in a relaxed manner and that's how you have to repeat the mantra.

The reading from *Durga Saptashati* will be repeated one hundred times during the five days of the yajna. Those people who will be participating in the chanting of Devi Path will be called 'Pathis' and will be provided with a copy of *Durga Saptashati*. You need not purchase it from the market. This is a rare privilege which you will seldom get at a yajna anywhere else. Elsewhere in India a yajna is a place for merrymaking, it is a show, but I must remind you that a yajna is neither a place for merrymaking, nor a show. This is a place for sadhana. Educated people from India and abroad have come here in large numbers to realize the subtle presence and to experience God, to obtain relief from their distress, sickness and other problems.

Conqueror of hearts

This is the first year of the Rajasooya Yajna. The Rajasooya Yajna is conducted by one who is a conqueror and I consider myself to be a conqueror. I have my own empire throughout the world. From 1964 until 1983, I conquered people's hearts and made them my own. Therefore, to celebrate my conquest the Rajasooya Yajna begins this year. It will continue for twelve years. The Rajasooya Yajna is performed over many years, not in one year. A yajna has three important parts. Firstly, the pooja, the tantric worship, the chanting and the ritual; secondly, satsang, kirtan and spiritual company; and thirdly, giving prasad to each and everyone. Giving means that you also give and I also give. This is yajna.

I have now decided that things will not improve by my staying silent. I regard myself as a *digvijayi*, one who has conquered the seven seas. From 1963 until 1983 I travelled to every corner of the world and established the flag of yoga. This was at a time when nobody knew about yoga. I took this ancient science and art of ours out of the forests and planted it in hospitals, schools and colleges. Yoga was transferred from the ashrams of the sages to dance institutes and music centres. I established yoga in the Christian community too. Everyone cooperated with me in this endeavour. No one challenged me. No one questioned my credentials, never!

East meets West

Once I met the Pope at the Vatican. When I told him I taught yoga, he remarked, "Yoga is an oriental philosophy and we are occidental. How will you integrate Eastern philosophy with Western culture?" I replied, "As was done two thousand years ago. As an oriental philosophy Christianity is firmly rooted in occidental culture. Similarly, yoga is an oriental science and it can also fit into occidental society." The Pope was silenced by my forthright reply. He knew that Christianity is an oriental religion. So my path was clear. All the important Christian centres welcomed me – Catholic and Protestant. Everywhere I was received with respect and assisted in every way.

Christianity was born in the East. Christ visited India and Nepal; he lived in Varanasi and Puri. He was initiated on Indian soil. The whole world knows it. Even if the church does not accept it, history records this fact. History says that Christ spent twelve years in India and the Bible bears this out, as it is silent about thirteen years of his life. Records relating to this period are found in the archives in Kathmandu and bear testimony to this historical fact. After all, what is Christianity? It is raja yoga. When Christ came to India some two thousand years ago there were two thought currents prevalent. One was Buddhism and the other was Vaishnavism. Buddha's philosophy was predominantly ethical whereas Vaishnava philosophy was predominantly devotional. Christianity embraces both.

My next sojourn was in South America and all the important Catholic monasteries had prior information about my visit. The Pope had instructed them to listen to Swami Satyananda and to give him every comfort. My line was clear and I was received everywhere from Colombia to Venezuela and Argentina. I visited many churches in those countries and taught the people yogic practices. Many devotees living there became sannyasins. I told them to follow their religion but to have their heads shaved, and they did. The bravest act in the world is to have someone shave their head. Only an intelligent man can accomplish this feat. A dullard can't

59

do it, as he will be easily trapped by others. If all of you were to have your heads shaved the poor barber would be able to maintain his family with the renumeration! Barbers also have to survive.

I gave each devotee a spiritual name. First Swami, second Ananda and third Saraswati – like Swami Rajrajananda Saraswati. Sometimes people asked me how they could distinguish between a female and a male just by knowing their spiritual name. Should the ladies be addressed as swamini? I said no! Sannyasins do not need to be categorized as male and female. Why do you need to know that? No swaminis, only swamis.

Devi is a mother

If you want to join in the flow of pooja during the yajna but cannot read *Durga Saptashati*, it doesn't matter. Just repeat mentally the mantra we have given you in a relaxed way, as if you are talking to a friend, because Devi is not a goddess, she's a mother. There is a difference between mother and goddess. The mother is she whom you are closest to. The goddess is she whom you have never seen. She is the mother and I am the child. She is full of forgiveness and I am full of mistakes. A child can become a bad child, but a mother can never become a bad mother. A child may become a hopeless child, a disastrous child, but a mother can never become a disastrous mother. She is a mother with tolerance, with forbearance, with eternal forgiveness, with compassion, with love for every child, whether blind or incapacitated, a thief or a criminal.

It is not an abstract approach, not an academic or philosophical approach, it is a very pragmatic approach. If she is a mother, then she has to be only a mother. And if she's a mother, then I have a right to her compassion, to her love, just as every child has a right to demand that from his mother. If she is not a mother, and if she is an abstract and formless goddess, then I don't know how to manage her. If she is abstract, then she has perhaps only a psycho-emotional reality for me, not a true reality. The approach of a spiritual aspirant towards God should be like the relationship between a child and a mother; it is the easiest.

Don't take your God away from you. I hope you understand this. Bring Him closer. Of course, if you bring God closest to you, then the principle is 'My Father and I are one', *Aham Brahmasmi, Analhak*. But that is not easily digestible. The easiest approach is that, perhaps next to myself, the closest to me is my mother. That is the concept of Devi, that is the concept of mother and that is the concept of true reality.

True reality is not an abstract reality. True reality is a reality. There is a difference between truth and reality. I am not talking about truth. The Vedas talk about truth. The Koran talks about truth. The Bible talks about truth. Swami Satyananda is talking to you about reality. Reality is always in connection with oneself. When I talk about reality, I am talking about something that is connected, related, associated with me. Truth is not something that is related to me. It is the truth, that's all it is. I don't challenge the truth. I don't challenge the Bible. I don't challenge any truth. Truth is truth. But there is something more important, which is called reality. The reality is that I need compassion, I need blessings, I need shelter, I need sympathy, I need help!

Diet for the yajna

As this is the first year of the Rajasooya Yajna, we have prepared puris, vegetables and some sweets, which is quite sattwic. You will not find boiled rice, bread, pulse, pulao or khichari here. This year the food has been prepared for this *anushthana*, this fixed course of sadhana. It is the appropriate food according to the scriptures. You will have to utter *'Namastasye Namastasye Namastasye Namo Namaha'* and *'Aim Hrim Klim'* for at least five or six hours. When you are repeating the mantras you are practising five hours of *rechaka*, exhalation, and five hours of *bhramari*, humming bee breath. This requires a lot of energy and hence we have puris, halwa and vegetables for you. You need some good solid food. If you think you can't digest it, take a little less, but have your meals twice a day. Then just come and sit down here and avoid leaving the enclosure as far as possible.

I came here at seven o'clock this morning and I can stay sitting here till twelve o'clock. I am seventy-eight. I can control my bladder because I have decided to, that's all! In the afternoon I will come again at one o'clock and leave at six o'clock. That's five hours. For a man of seventy-eight it is very difficult. Ask these old men how much difficulty they are having because they have not made the decision to stay here. I have decided I will stay here and have kidney control, not kidney prakshalana!

We have made no arrangement for those who only want to eat fruit. I do not understand its significance. It may be appropriate for Ekadashi, the eleventh day of the full moon, but not for this exercise of repeating mantras a hundred times. This is the first year of the Rajasooya Yajna and you will not get bread here. You can have the food of your choice in hotels, both vegetarian and non-vegetarian, but you will only get puris here. You may eat once a day if you cannot take more, but it is better to eat just half the amount twice a day. Instead of taking twenty-five or thirty puris, take ten. Why do you laugh? When I was young I used to eat thirty or forty of them! Puris are so small.

This year people were all wonder-struck at the menu. They said, "What are you doing? There is no pulao." I replied, "This is the first year of the Rajasooya Yajna. Next year you will have many more varieties. In the Rajasooya Yajna a time comes when from sunrise to sunset anyone who comes is given food, whether it is a man, a cow, a cock, a pig or a bird. That is called *langar*, serving free food to all. When you feed a hundred thousand people a day you should not feed rice, because it can cause food poisoning if it is not eaten quite soon after cooking. As far as meat goes, you know about mad cow disease. In any case, beef is not a pure food. Beef is something that one day or another our civilization must get rid of. It is dangerous to man's survival. We know that very well. There is no use just killing all the cattle, you just have to kill that habit. There are many other good things to eat!

Language of love

Today is the concluding day of the rasalila festival. I believe that there are things in life that don't need language to be interpreted. That is the language of satyam, shivam and sundaram. Love cannot be understood just in English. It is all beautiful – their lips were sweet, their bodies were sweet, their language and expression were sweet, their movements were sweet. Everything about the Lord is nothing but sweet. The total is love.

We still long to see such a man as Krishna descending to earth. Krishna was a great teacher. That was the period when he had absolute time with Radha, and you know how tender he was with Radha. He did not behave like a man, he behaved like her disciple. He bowed down to her first, and then they were totally in love with each other. Even today we do not remember anyone except Radha and Krishna. We don't remember any of Krishna's other wives. We don't say, "Satya bhama Krishna, bhanumati Krishna," we say, "Radha-Krishna," because that is the relationship with the spirit within us. If you happen to go to Vrindavan, particularly in the month of Shravan, the end of July to mid August, you will find a lot of rasalila there.

Holi in Barsana

Swami Niranjan: Now we are going to witness a depiction of Holi played between Nandgaon and Barsana. Barsana, near Mathura, was the birthplace of Radha and every year she would invite Krishna and the cowherd boys to come and play Holi. In Barsana, Holi is played on the ninth day of the lunar calendar month of Phalgun, which corresponds approximately to March according to the Gregorian calendar. Then on the tenth day of Phalgun Holi is played in Nandgaon. On the eleventh day it is played in Vrajadham. So Holi is played on three days.

As you know, Holi is the festival of colours. Even today people throughout India enjoy this festival of colours in which they drench each other in bright colours. It is a festival of joy and happiness. There is one unique aspect of the Holi

63

that is played in Barsana. According to the tradition, before playing Holi the young girls are fed sumptuously for three months, so that they become strong and hefty. They are given a lot of ghee, butter, milk and rich foods full of protein, so that on the day of Holi all the girls can bash all the boys with long wooden sticks or *lathis*.

Even today thousands go to Barsana to witness Holi. People go from Nandgaon, the birthplace of Krishna, to Barsana in the morning. It is a distance of about fourteen kilometres and they run all the way. When they reach Barsana, the roads there are very narrow. In some places the road is only five feet wide, in others it is about seven feet wide. The boys have to run through these narrow lanes. In each gateway there is a hefty gopi standing with a stick and they beat the boys who have to defend themselves with a shield. This Holi is played for about two hours. It is a very tough Holi known as Lathmar Holi, Holi with sticks.

Festival of bliss

Sri Swamiji: In India we have four main festivals. Holi is a major festival. We don't talk about Republic Day or Independence Day very much. The second major festival is Diwali, the festival of light. The third is Dussehra, which is celebrated to remember the conquest of Rama over Ravana, and the fourth is Raksha Bandhana, the festival of the thread of love and affection between brothers and sisters. Holi is a festival of happiness. But it is not merely a festival of mirth and joy, it is the festival of ananda. Ananda is neither happiness, nor absence of happiness. We are all anandam. This is not social happiness, mental happiness or psychological happiness. This is the happiness which emerges when you become as innocent as a child. No intellect, no buddhi, no guilt. You are free. You are neither a man nor a woman. In Lord Krishna is depicted the completeness of human life right from childhood to knowledge of the *Srimad Bhagavad Gita*.

Rasalila is a festival of supreme happiness, supreme bliss. This happiness transcends pleasure and pain. The Upanishads say, *Rasam hi eva ayam labdhva anandi bhavati* – "The

64

individual ego receiving the nectar of consciousness becomes eternal." Again they declare, *Raso vasah* – "That (supreme consciousness) is verily rasa (nectar)." God is supreme bliss. God is not at all dry. God is supreme bliss incarnate. For this reason I often say that our Vedic religion is polytheistic and that I have had an encounter with the Godhead. In our scheme of things we realize God in the shape of a statue. We perceive God in the form of the guru. We see God moving about, eating and drinking, sleeping and waking, and ailing too. This has a mystic aspect too.

All the religions of the world believing in one God have given birth to violence because their philosophies have political overtones. Don't forget that religion and philosophy have far-reaching consequences. They can give birth to violence. The non-dualistic Vedic religion that we pursue generates peace, non-violence, love, comradeship and brotherhood. Spirituality and philosophy, not social factors, are responsible for the development and growth of brotherhood and peace. For this reason our great sages and seers have always said, *Eko Brahma dwitiyo nasti* – "God is only one, without a second," which led to people worshipping Lord Krishna in human form. Today we have worshipped the deity in the form of Krishna and in the form of Radha. We have not worshipped them as human beings. No, we have never done that.

You were all so happy when holy water was being sprin- kled on you for Holi. You felt as of Lord Krishna himself was drizzling consecrated water over your heads. This is the feeling of a small child. Jesus Christ also said, "Don't be childish, be childlike."

Swami Niranjan: The presentation of the enchanting rasalila has brought glory to Rikhiadham and to the people at large. The exploits of Lord Krishna and the glimpses of his chequered life have been very powerfully depicted by the accomplished artists from the Rasalila Institute and we have all benefited greatly. I offer my thanks and respect to all the artists on my own behalf and on behalf of all the people gathered here. I offer my special respects and regards to Swami Hara Govinda Maharaj who has very kindly brought his Rasalila troupe to this far-flung place. He is the spirit behind this glorious event and we hope he will be with us again in the future to bring alive the nectar of Krishna's life.

Sri Swamiji: The festival began on Tuesday, a day that has a special significance in our tradition, and we hope that this will be a good omen and bring us blessings. May this occasion bestow upon us bountiful blessings in happiness and despair, in plenty and adversity, in all conditions.

Satsang 7

December 15, 2001, Morning

We have assembled here in connection with the Sat Chandi Yajna of the first year of the Rajasooya Yajna and we pray to God for the peace, plenty and prosperity of everyone. We pray to the Mother to give us the wisdom to live properly. In whatever condition you keep us it does not matter. Give us the wisdom to face this life. Give us the strength to bear this life. This is what we need. We need the blessings, the protection, the grace and the compassion of Mother. After the chanting of Ramacharitamanas Path, the pandits and acharyas will begin the process of installing the deity and the flag post has already been erected.

On the holy occasion of this yajna, we have resolved to distribute prasad to the rural families of Rikhia, to the elderly, to the widows, to the Santhalis who have been associated with this akhara since its inception and who have cooperated unfailingly with us in all our efforts over the past ten to twelve years. We have further resolved to give prasad to the sannyasins, who have come from every nook and corner of the world, from east, west, north and south, from every dimension and from every religion, who have contributed a lot to dharma and to spiritual life. During these four days prasad will be distributed to all the participants in this yajna.

Sannyasins

The sannyasins come from different countries, ethnic groups, religions and cultures. They are not only from the Hindu religious tradition but from other religious backgrounds too. They have dedicated their whole lives to the cause of yoga. They are a highly educated and accomplished group of people and have rich experience in the fields of culture and civilization. They are not babas. Each one of you should remember this. I am specifically referring to the people of this panchayat. Let it be known that we are not babas as people generally think. Some of the sannyasins are not only computer engineers but have knowledge of missile technology too. Such highly qualified and talented sannyasins have come to participate in this yajna. Some who design high tech weapons, high power bombers and jet fighters have joined us as sannyasins for the occasion. I have told them plainly, "If the world is to survive, if society is to be rebuilt, then industry alone is not enough." In response to my call they have come from all over India and the world to participate in this yajna.

They are not traditional babas; they are sannyasins of the Dashnami tradition, the order established by Adi Guru Shankaracharya and they are associated with the Vedic tradition, thought and culture. Many of them were born during my time, so they have had a long association with this tradition from childhood. They will all receive gifts today. Nobody should leave without prasad. Some have come here from far off places at our request. It is, therefore, essential and incumbent upon us to receive them, to welcome them and to honour them.

A society is built on righteousness, the family is built by following the path of righteousness. If religion is swept away, your wife will not remain your wife, your husband will not remain your husband, your father and your son will not remain your father and son. Dharma is the only binding force and as such, first of all it has to be re-established. It could be re-established in the name of Sri Rama, for Rama was the incarnation of dharma. Rama represented propriety

68

and rectitude. He lived his whole life as a son, a husband, a father, a king, a subject and a warrior. This is why I have initiated the yajna in his name.

Empire of the heart

This is the first year of the Rajasooya Yajna, which will now be conducted every year for twelve years. Sri Rama and King Yudhishthira also performed the Rajasooya Yajna. In Yudhishthira's Rajasooya Yajna, Sri Krishna undertook to wash the guest's feet and to collect the leftovers and leaf plates used in feeding the people. This is the same Rajasooya Yajna. Only a world conqueror is qualified to perform the Rajasooya Yajna. Empires can be acquired in two ways. One is by means of the sword or the gun with the assistance of the army and the other is by winning over the people's hearts. This is an empire of the heart. To win people's hearts is a great thing, it is not a joke. The seers and sages are duty bound to win over the world. Adi Guru Shankaracharya was credited with conquering the world one thousand five hundred years ago, as was Swami Vivekananda. Lord Buddha could not achieve this distinction during his lifetime. Buddhism became universal after his death, spreading throughout the length and breadth of the globe.

In the same way Swami Satyananda of Rikhia is also a world conqueror. No religion, no country, city or town has challenged me on this score. I have received respect and unqualified support for my efforts everywhere. It is unique that I am acceptable to one and all. This is also one of the characteristics of a world conqueror. My ashrams are dotted all over the Christian world. I have initiated many young people belonging to different religious groups into the sannyasa order using Vedic mantras, No one ever challenged me because I possess something very valuable, which is the blessing of my guru.

I served my guru, Swami Sivananda, for twelve years without a break when I was a young man. It is the duty of disciples to work for their guru; it is the duty of a son to manage his father's affairs. I asked my guru to remain seated, that we would construct the ashram, print the books, do everything. He was not to worry about all these jobs. I received his blessings in full measure.

I had also received clear directions from my parents. My parents told me not to retaliate even if someone hit me, not to bear ill will against anyone, because it is a weak spot in one's character. Only the weak and cowards bear ill will and have fits of anger, only the weak-hearted take up cudgels and fire arms. What is the weapon of those who are strong and powerful? It is not forgiveness, it is love. I have received profound love from childhood.

I have also never asked for anything in my life, not from anyone. I never demand anything from anyone. Demanding is not my creed, begging is not my creed. I know how to write, how to speak, how to think. One who can write, speak and think can rule the world. My books have sold very well throughout the world and are printed in many languages – Hindi, English, French, German, Russian, Italian and Spanish.

Chandi Yajna

Mother Chandi and Lord Ganesha are very important deities in this industrial age. They find support in the scriptures too. In Kali Yuga these deities have become very important. This Sat Chandi Yajna is very powerful. The chanting of mantras is very correct and pure and the ground where you are sitting has been sanctified. The presiding deity of this surrounding area has been invoked. There has been chanting, kirtans and bhajans and the entire area has been purified. This property is named Tapowan and all the buildings and structures erected here have been designed and fashioned strictly according to the norms prescribed by the Vastu shastras, the ancient science of architecture.

This yajna is based on the tantric system. A hundred rounds of this worship will be conducted during these five days, twenty rounds per day. Today you will be free at twelve and you will be expected back again at two, but tomorrow there will be a very short interval between ten and eleven.

Within that period you will have to manage everything, including your lunch. This yajna will be officially closed on the nineteenth. The priests conducting the yajna have come from Varanasi and have been associated with me for many years. Pandit Bhatnagarji started coming to Munger when he was very young. His superior also used to come to Munger when I was there long ago. In Munger we also used to have Sat Chandi Yajna.

India is the country of yajnas. Although hundreds of thousands of yajnas are performed each year in India, the tradition of the yajna performed in Rikhia has quite a different angle. Even in Deoghar you may have seen yajnas, but in most places there is not enough space to accommodate everyone. Here the yajna will be held in perfect peace. People will remain seated during the yajna. On that side over five hundred people are seated with books and malas in their hands ready to participate in the chanting. One hundred and fifty are from the nearby villages and the remainder from outside the area. You can see the multitude of devotees from overseas sitting on the other side. Rikhia residents do not believe in rowdiness on the sacred occasion of Devi Pooja. In our yajna there is no noise or disorder, no festivities or show. In a civilized society a yajna should be able to be performed in a civilized manner.

Tradition of giving during yajna

In the tradition followed in the Rajasooya Yajna, there are three essentials. The first is worship of the deity, which means sitting and singing the praises of God, doing kirtan or listening to the glorious exploits of Godheads. The second includes the ritualistic installation, the chanting of mantras etc. The third is giving and receiving. The yajna cannot be complete without daan or giving. This was the tradition when Sri Rama ruled the earth. The tradition was followed during the Dwapara period and the same tradition should also be followed during the present age, Kali Yuga. In Kali Yuga, however, the pandits have deviated from the tradition and instead of giving they have become used to taking. The

71

brahmins and pandits receive things in the form of dakshina. They form societies and associations and collect some forty to fifty thousand rupees, spend a part of the huge collection on performing the yajna and save the rest for their own use.

There is a clear provision for giving in the Rajasooya Yajna. According to the tradition provision for donation has been made in the first, second and third years of the yajna. Beyond the third year there is provision for giving away food grains. Giving away food grains means providing a free meal kitchen, *anna kshetra*. All sorts of people come to the free meal kitchen which starts from the third or the fifth year. This is guided by two types of rulers. According to the tradition, all the kings who had been vanquished by Sri Rama and Yudhishthira came to the yajna and offered gifts to the conqueror king who in turn gave away gifts to the vanquished kings. We have decided to follow the same tradition because whatever is given to us as gifts we return as prasad.

Share your wealth

The prasad will be distributed to the villagers first, as they are our distinguished guests. Those who will distribute the prasad are blessed ones. To give prasad is a meritorious act and to offer prasad is a person's first religious obligation. Let me tell you one episode. Once upon a time there was a thunderous sound in the firmament. The sound was 'Da' repeated three times. The sages and seers who were assembled heard the uproar and asked what the sound indicated. One said it meant three things: first to give, second to subdue or suppress, and third to show mercy, to be kind.

Someone asked for an explanation of the import of these three words. Then the reply came. Human beings should share their earnings and give to others because they are inherently tight-fisted and miserly. Demons should be kind and show mercy to others as they are very cruel and devilish by nature. Devas are pleasure seekers and should restrain their passions. So, the devas need to exercise restraint, the demons need to be kind and compassionate to all and human beings need to share their earnings with those who are deprived and less fortunate.

You all belong to the miserly class and so the prasad will be given away to the deserving people through your hands. You will break your record of sitting tight on your earnings and savings. First let the children come forward to distribute the prasad and learn the basic lesson of giving to others. To give, to donate, to share your bread with your less fortunate brothers and sisters is the loftiest ideal of life. The worst type of meanness and pettiness is to sit tight on your possessions. The most despicable part of human character is to crave everything and not share your wealth with others. Try and learn to give to others. You have not learnt this noble ideal so far. I am not referring to the children. I am referring to the adults who are very miserly.

Old age

I am not against drinking but drinking is definitely not good for us. However, even if you drink, God will come to you. God does not hate drinkers. God does not hate smokers. God does not hate anyone. God does not punish anyone. The old age pensioners have a few years left at their disposal, but their children don't give them any money for smoking and drinking. So I decided to give them twelve hundred rupees a year. That's not enough, but at least they can smoke bidis. I don't believe that if you want to have the darshan of God you should have to give up bidis. Giving up smoking is not a precondition for realizing God. There is no code that says you have to give up smoking to have oneness with God. Of course, smoking can damage your heart, lungs and throat. You may get cancer, which will be fatal, but when it comes to God-realization, it is not essential to give up bidi and cigarette smoking, eating meat and drinking wine. No doubt these things are bad for the health and you should give them up for your good health and well-being.

We are sadhus and sannyasins, we have to show you the way. We have to draw your attention to the good and bad side of something and leave it up to you make a decision in your own interests. We also have to show you how to attain oneness with God and to publicize the pitfalls too. But old age has its own code of conduct. Elderly people, those who are over sixty, overstep the restrictions. We have a certain code of conduct here which they do not understand. If we ask them to sit down, they stand up and if we ask them to stand up, they sit down.

Culture of give and take

Yajna has three components: worship of God, ritual and giving. These practices have been followed from time immemorial. Numerous yajnas are held in India. Whatever the quality, yajna is yajna. But people go to the yajnashala and return empty-handed. Nothing happens there. In our yajna you will find all three components. In the early morning you have worship of the deity. This morning you participated in Ramacharitamanas chanting. We also had kirtan. Worship of the deity will continue for the whole day. We will have a two hour recess, which will be reduced to one hour from tomorrow, as the chanting will be repeated one hundred times.

The third component is giving. The poor, the impoverished and the affluent all have to participate in the yajna. This time we have put the children in the forefront, because they are the up and coming generation. We will have the prasad distributed from their hands as we wish to banish meanness from our society. By and large people are very tight-fisted and you know that miserliness is the weakest point in man's character. Therefore, children should learn early in life how to share their pleasure with their fellow beings. They should imitate the habit of giving. Giving good samskaras in the formative years will bring about changes in their attitude to life. That is why I have chosen the children.

The society which knows only one culture, the culture of receiving and not giving, promotes social exploitation. To strike a balance in society we should teach children to follow the culture of give and take. Your parents teach you only to receive and take from others. They must teach you to give as well. I am not saying you should only teach them to give.

74

No, that is not my point. If we don't receive from others, how can we give? We should strike a balance between the two and only then can social balance be sustained. Unless this social balance is achieved, the gap between affluence and poverty cannot be bridged.

We should, therefore, train our children to strike a balance between giving and taking. If you earn a lot, you must spend too. If your child earns three thousand rupees a month, he spends two thousand on domestic requirements and puts a thousand into fixed deposit. Ask him to spend a few rupees on others also. If you don't give to others how will you get anything back. If you purchase something from a shop, the transaction is complete only when you have paid. You purchase a utensil from a shop and pay for it. The shopkeeper goes to market and purchases food and clothing with that earning. This is how society runs and there is a social balance. To keep this element of social balance, provision has been made in the yajna for daan, giving of prasad.

We do not call prasad donation or alms. We call it honour. We have deleted the words donation and alms from our dictionary. Today we will honour the village folk first, then the elderly people and then the widows. Then come the Santhali labourers who have worked ceaselessly for twelve long years to construct this ashram. Then it will be the turn of the revenue officials of the survey and settlement wing of the state government working in this area. Lastly the sannyasins will be honoured.

Spreading the message of yoga

Sannyasins have a big role to play in society. The so-called babas will not improve the quality of social life. The babas have outlived their life. Now society requires good quality sannyasins. Two thousand years ago Adi Guru Shankaracharya established the Dashnami order of sannyasa. We are maintaining the heritage of that sannyasa order. These sannyasins have done a wonderful job. They have travelled the world and have preached the message of yoga in every

75

nook and corner. No country or island has remained untouched. No city, town or village has not received the message of yoga. The credit for this goes to one person in the twentieth century and that one person is Swami Satyananda who is sitting in your midst. Everyone helped me and success dawned at the fag end of the twentieth century.

Let me tell you one episode. I always travelled first class, never second class. My secretary used to accompany me on my tours abroad. My meals of Indian puris and vegetables would come from five star hotels. I always lived with dignity. Sometimes when my luggage was checked in at the airport it would weigh one hundred kilos and the maximum limit is thirty kilos. When the airways officials objected, I would tell them to close their eyes, and they would laugh. In this way I was able to carry my books and malas. I am talking of my early tours abroad. People abroad used to shower love and affection on me.

The following episode is especially reminiscent of the degree of cooperation I received. Once, while returning from South America on the last leg of my tour, I was carrying a suitcase full of bundles of dollar notes. When I arrived in Frankfurt, the customs officials checked my suitcase and immediately asked, "Have you come to purchase Germany?" I replied, "If it is possible to purchase Germany with this amount I am ready to strike the deal!" Thus I obtained the cooperation of customs clearance people all over the world. They never created any obstacles. Custom regulations exist and customs officers embarrass many big wigs, ministers and diplomats, but I was never given a grilling.

The right education

I always followed the instruction of my parents. This instruction was, "My child, you are born a kshatriya, a warrior. Your ancestors ruled over the world with a sword, but you have to resort to humility and modesty. The world will be conquered through humility, not with the sword. But now the world has changed. Whoever bends low goes higher and higher. Nobody has the inclination to lie low, but once you tend to lie low you will reach the highest peak! This was the first lesson I received.

The second lesson I received at my guru's ashram. My guru put me in charge of everything in the ashram. I was of a tender age then. At school I had learnt the names of the daughters of Akbar and Aurangzeb. Tell me, could you earn your livelihood with that education? Could you build your house with that knowledge? That is the kind of education you get at school, but at my guru's ashram I had the right kind of education.

The lessons I learnt at my parents' home and at my guru's ashram helped me to build up my future. I did not behave roughly with anyone. I was always modest and humble in my behaviour. I know that one who can bow can bend others. I tell you all to be kind and considerate. This world deserves compassion and kindness, not recriminations and reprisals. If you look into the past of those who are impolite and impertinent, you will find that they have been wronged. Maybe their parents were unjust or society harassed them.

Cloth – the greatest gift in the world

I learnt about the importance of clothing from Mahatma Gandhi when I was a child of eight or nine. Gandhi was my childhood saint. I was born in 1923 and by 1930–31 I knew what leaders like Mahatma Gandhi were saying. I was then seven or eight years old. Gandhi said that India would win freedom by means of a *charkha*, a spinning wheel. How could a charkha bring independence to the country? The whole country was seething with this question. People used to ridicule Gandhi because they thought that freedom could be won only through gunpowder, violence and bloody revolution. But Gandhi stood his ground. He said, "No guns, no rifles, no violence." When I asked, "Who is this Gandhiji?" I was told, *Aaya Gandhi, aaya andhi* – "Gandhi has come and he has brought upheaval." As a child I used to chant slogans like this and it created an indelible imprint on my mind.

Gandhi used to say that you can manage to go without food for a day or two, but you can't do without clothes for even a minute. Can any of you go without clothes for a minute? Can you undress yourself even for a second in the public gaze? No, you can't do it. Cloth is the life companion of a human being. The greatest gift in the world is cloth. Gandhi associated people with khadi clothes to win their hearts. I have also done the same thing.

Many people force widows to wear white clothes. This rite will not hold good here. We follow the normal practice and you will not be able to distinguish a widow from a married woman on the basis of their clothing. I cannot appreciate the social custom of widow and widower. My mind does not accept it. Widows are directed not to wear good clothes and ornaments. In my view everyone should have his or her own choice in matters of clothing and social behaviour. Everyone should have the right to live his or her life according to his or her choice. Society should not impose unreasonable restraints on them.

When Gandhi stepped into the freedom movement he did not take up arms or take recourse to weapons. He took up the spinning wheel and thread. This is part of history. People did not believe that the country could win freedom by spinning thread and making khadi clothes. Doubting Thomases thought that freedom could be won only by means of weapons. But Gandhi was firm in his resolve and he convinced the people that the country could win freedom only through non-violence and truth, and undoubtedly khadi thread would represent and symbolize non-violence.

The prasad of this yajna will be clothing because you live in association with clothes day and night. Do you follow the idea behind it? I have therefore procured clothing from Jammu and Kashmir, from Lucknow, from Assam, from Kerala and from West Bengal. I have procured clothes from every part of India. The storehouse is full of clothes which I will distribute to all of you. The pandits will also receive clothes. The affluent, those wallowing in wealth, will also receive clothes as prasad. I will offer clothes to the poor and destitute, to everyone who has come here, as clothes are worn by everyone. You should not complain that sweets and dried fruits were not offered as prasad.

Service to the Mother

Copies of the *Durga Saptashati* are being distributed. Those who are participating in the day long recitation may join the queue to receive copies of the book. Everyone should learn how to recite the *Durga Saptashati* and then participate in the recitation. When you enter this world you have to pass through the phases of pain and pleasure. Even if you wallow in pleasure and plenty, you are bound to pass through a phase of worry and anxiety, fear and apprehension. Granted you have wealth and affluence, but still there is fear lurking in your mind. How to get rid of this fear and worry? Devi relieves you of psychological and unfounded fears. You become free and fearless. So you must recite the *Saptashati* in your homes.

The recitation of *Durga Saptashati* will continue for five days. You are being given the duty of Mother Bhagavati for five days. This duty enjoins service to Mother Bhagavati. You may take it as a service to the Mother Goddess. You should imbibe the feeling of service. The spirit of service to Mother should be the guiding force behind your recitation. You should never have the feeling of ego, that you are doing a great thing by joining the recitation session. You should have the feeling of humility, not arrogance, not feeling superior to others. We should serve the Mother with the same spirit of dedication as servants serve their masters. We are all here to serve the Mother. I don't say recitation of *Durga Saptashati,* I say service to Mother. So now Devi is being installed. The installation will be over by twelve o'clock and at two we will start the recitation, the service to the Mother.

79

Satsang 8

December 15, 2001, Afternoon

*J*ust see how God sends people from unknown quarters to fulfil the desires of His devotees. When I decided to give earrings to all the rural women, the idea struck someone living far away from here and he sent an e-mail offering me three thousand pairs or earrings. This is not a small offering, it's a big consignment. This is the first year of the Rajasooya Yajna and we have received this large offering. Maybe in the concluding year of Rajasooya we will receive gold and diamonds. Who can say?

It is God who sends and it is God who receives. This is not an impossible preposition. We are just instruments. We came with a bundle of karmas and we will return leaving the karmas behind. We will take nothing back with us. Whatever we earn here will have to be left behind. Tell me, will you take anything with you when you leave this world? When you proceed on your final journey you do not carry your earthly acquisitions. No material wealth, no land or cattle go with you. You leave behind the cars, the fleets of vehicles. You also leave behind your wife. Your wife goes with you only to the doorstep and your physical body accompanies you only to the burial ground. Only meritorious deeds performed during this lifetime go with you on your last journey. Everyone meets the same fate. Sometimes we live in

80

a fool's paradise and boast of our worldly possessions, but actually we are not great. We become insignificant when reduced to ashes. We come empty-handed and we will return empty-handed. In between if we acquire something we claim to be the sole owner and boast, "This is mine." But the fact is that this nest belongs neither to you nor to me; it is like the resting place of a bird.

Santhali workers

We call the masons *vishwakarmas,* or divine builders, because they have built the ashram. We used to procure coal from Dhanbad and make bricks here. Then we realized that the bricks made at Sultanganj were cheaper and harder then the ones we prepared here and so we decided to procure bricks from Sultanganj. Sultanganj bricks are so strong and long lasting that ten inch thick walls are not necessary, as even five inch thick walls will carry the weight of the foundation. The foundations, the columns and the roof are all done by these masons, as well as the outer and inner finishes. They have also installed the electrical fittings and two transformers in our ashram.

We don't call experts to install or maintain this equipment. These masons live within a radius of a few kilometres from the ashram. Electricians, carpenters and plumbers all live in the neighbourhood. Our sewage system is one of the best and has been designed and constructed by the local plumbers and masons. The water that we use is drained into underground pools and does not leave our premises. These people also look after the horticulture and gardening. They have planted all the teak trees, the white and black sheshems, the Assam bamboos and the neem plants. We do not plant trees for commercial purposes but for the sake of creating greenery to maintain an ecological balance.

Now the school teachers are receiving prasad. The next group will be the builders. The chief of this group is a Muslim gentleman. He is totally illiterate and does not know how to do accounting, so we do it all for him. He is the actual builder of this akhara. The Santhalis have done all the construction work here for the past twelve years. They are very honest and hardworking, but very independent. Their character is more European or Western than Indian. Indian labourers indulge in pilfering and smoke bidis during working hours. They are shirkers too, but the Santhalis do not shirk work. Because of their character their quality of work is superior. They have built this big hall and all the other buildings too, as well as digging wells and all types of other work. Their work is very neat and clean. We never have to worry whether or not they will turn up when required. If coal arrives from Dhanbad at night they come to unload it. That is why we hold them in high esteem.

Equal pay

We do not discriminate between male and female workers here. In the past the daily rate was eighteen rupees for men and sixteen rupees for women. When I asked why eighteen rupees for men and only sixteen for women, I was told it was the practice prevalent in this area. I said, "Let the practice go to the dogs. Women work harder than men and their output is greater than men's. So why should we pay women less?" Thereafter men and women have been paid equally in this ashram. I do not discriminate. At that time I used to pay them eighteen rupees. Now the daily wage has gone up to sixty rupees.

Here is Fakku, my oldest disciple in Rikhia. When I first came here she was a small child. Now she has grown up and married. If I need anything, I just contact her and she gets it for me. She is Swami Satsangi's best friend. This is Swabati. In 1989 she was eleven years old. The Santhalis are a peculiar mixture of tribalism, Hinduism and Christianity.

Bihar Yoga Bharati

I arrived in Rikhia on twenty-third September 1989, when day and night were equal. After I had been here for ten days, the work commenced. Astrologers have indicated in my horoscope that wherever I go, I will construct houses. On my parents' property I constructed houses and when I

82

started living in my guru's ashram in Rishikesh I did the same thing. Now Sivananda Ashram in Rishikesh is like a city. During my time in Munger I continued constructing and the fort-like building which now houses the Bihar Yoga Bharati University was erected during my time there. BYB is the first university of yoga in the world. There are universities of sport and music in the world but none are devoted solely to yoga.

Yoga is the oldest heritage of the world dating back to the time of Lord Shiva. Shiva was a yogi. But there was no proper university in the world to promote yogic studies and research. When we initiated a yoga university at Munger, the Chairman of the University Grants Commission remarked that it was a great thing for India as well as for the world that someone had conceived the idea of establishing a fully-fledged university of yoga. The degrees and diplomas granted by this university have been recognized all over the world. Students from far off places around the globe come to study yogic science in this university, as they did when the Nalanda University of Bihar's golden days was in existence. The Vikramshila and Takshashila universities of yoga also attracted students from different parts of the world. In the same way students from Korea, Colombia, Russia, Latvia, Iran and many other countries around the world come to Bihar Yoga Bharati, Munger, to study yogic sciences. This is a very big achievement for Munger.

Contribution of sannyasins

A sannyasin has to learn how to live with everyone, to accommodate thieves and cheats, vagabonds and social outcasts, good and bad people. A sannyasin has to live with men and women, young and old without any distinctions. He has to remain above all this and that is his achievement. Under my leadership many of the sannyasins renounced their youth for the sake of yoga. Had they not joined us to serve the cause of yoga, I could not have gone so far in my vision. Now yoga has received universal acceptance. Had my sannyasins from far off lands not spearheaded the

83

movement of yoga, it could have died like many other movements.

I have created a large number of sannyasins who have sacrificed their careers for the cause of yoga. They are fully committed to yoga. It is a big thing; their sacrifice is great. Many are highly qualified in different fields of knowledge. Some are scientists and work in big scientific laboratories in their homelands for five or six months a year, earn a lot of money and then come back to work for us and enjoy their life as sadhus and sannyasins. Some are master musicians too. They also organize and conduct kirtans in an effective manner. But all have dedicated their life to sannyasa.

There was a lack of educational institutions in India and so when the Europeans invaded India, Christian schools sprang up in every corner of the country. Even so, in Western countries there was a lack of spiritual centres and so spiritual centres have started proliferating. Western countries are already saturated with schools and convents, but yogic and spiritual centres are not in existence. They badly need yoga and spirituality, bhajan and kirtan, asana and pranayama, and are importing these things from India. I tell them to open yoga schools and centres and I will provide yoga teachers.

Some of the sannyasins have also received a talisman, a *tabiz*, as prasad. The talisman has been consecrated. It is not a locket, it is a Sri Yantra tabiz to provide protection from *asuric* or evil forces. Sannyasins need protection from asuric forces. It is only we in India who use the tabiz for protection against external and internal evil forces, mystical negative forces.

Yantra, mantra and mandala – symbols of divine energy
Look at the symbolic representation of the Devi. It is a yantric symbol of Devi, not an idol or statue. According to tantra and according to the mystic sciences, there are three important symbols of divine energy known as mantra, yantra and mandala. These are the three symbols of God, the three symbols of formless reality. These three forms are *mantra*,

which is sound; *yantra,* which is a geometrical diagram; and *mandala,* which is in the form of a statue, of a shivalinga, or anything that has the three dimensions of depth, width and height. An object that has dimensions is called a mandala. I have dimensions, I am a mandala.

Yantra is a geometrical formation. The triangle, or *trikona* as we call it, is very important. This triangle is so organized and so placed that it becomes the cosmic yantra. The cosmic yantra is known as Sri Yantra. Many of you will be receiving the Sri Yantra as prasad. I have given it as your talisman. In fact it is a very peculiar concept of physics. Scientists now feel that the universe is a play of matter, and this matter can be broken into atoms, molecules, etc. But we say something else. We say there are invisible things in this universe which are in the form of geometrical formations, and these geometrical formations are the ultimate formation of the whole universe. This means the whole universe is a mathematical reality, a geometrical reality. That is yantra, and it is not a simple science.

In tantric literature, there is *vama marga,* left hand tantra, and *dakshina marga,* right hand tantra. This is right hand tantra, not left hand tantra. In right hand tantra the Sri Yantra has the Devi, which is the feminine form. In fact the feminine aspect of reality, the feminine aspect of creation, is always symbolized by a triangle. That triangle is called yoni chakra. I am giving you a very superficial outline only because we are talking of something which is really subtle, which is beyond the mind, which is beyond matter. We are talking about something which is not an object, which is not the subject matter of the eyes or the ears. It is something which mystics do experience at a certain level of consciousness, otherwise not! It is logical. Can you dream now? No you can't dream now. You cannot develop, you cannot manifest, you cannot project. You cannot bring about a dream experience now because you are not in that state of consciousness. I am just giving you an example. In the same way unless you bring about a change in the realm of consciousness, in the quality of consciousness, unless you

85

are able to unfold that layer of reality, you can't have that experience which we call yantra, geometrical mantra.

So our gurus and acharyas said, "First open the layer of mind. Develop your consciousness. Develop your awareness. Develop that state of consciousness where you can see the sound. Develop that state of mind where you can experience a sound in its subtle form. It is with that purpose that they will be establishing the *vigraha,* the concrete external form, of Mother, of Devi. That is the tantric reality. You have often heard about tantra. This entire worship is tantric. It is based on the rules of agama. You have heard of agama shastra and nigama shastra. This is agama shastra. The sound is the sound of mantra. Sound is the revealed reality. That is nothing new to any of us. Christians say the Bible is revealed, Muslims say the Koran is revealed and Hindus say the Vedas are revealed. What does it mean? The sound is heard in the depths of consciousness.

Our inner form
This is a superficial introduction to this tantric pooja. The acharyas will continue this *sthapana,* this complete installation, for one hour. They will purify the atmosphere, the pillars, the flag and everything else. These things have a meaning. That little place where they are now represents yourself. You are there, that is you. It is the pavilion of Devi, but it is not a pavilion. It is your subtle form, it is you. This pavilion represents you. The pillars of the pavilion, the land and the superstructure symbolize us. We are there. Here we are in the form of a physical body. This is a cage; this is not our physical form. That is our mystic form, our spiritual form, our inner form. The pooja being performed there is being done in our inner self.

The scriptures declare, *Deho devalayah proktah jeevo devah sanatanah* – "This human body is a temple and this living being is an immortal god within it." This body, this physical form, is a temple, a sanctum sanctorum, a place of worship, a place of God, a place of reality. This body is the abode of the soul, the abode of God, the abode of the purusha. They have this regard for the human body. The god residing in this body is the human being. An immortal god resides within this being. That god is always there; he is there today and he will be there tomorrow. That which exists all the time, which does not cease to exist, is called *sanatan*, eternal. That soul or spirit resides there all the time and that soul is the God.

The truth has been represented there in the form of a mandap. This yajna mandap where you are sitting is the symbolic representation of the human body. Now you can say that this human body is the pavilion where the yajna is being performed. The *karta*, the doer, of this yajna is 'I' and the *devata*, the divine being, of this yajna is 'you'. You should sit in the yajna mandap with this feeling in your mind. Even in the pooja mandap you should sit with this feeling.

However, the truth of the matter is that nobody can explain it to you fully. Neither can I explain the full implications of the yajna, nor would you understand it. Frankly speaking, if you were to understand the full implications of the truth, then what would be left? There would be no truth left. So, whatever we say in respect of truth, we say for the sake of pleasure, for the sake of our satisfaction and understanding. We say so to generate bliss and happiness. The urge to discourse about God comes from my inner self. The urge comes to hear about God. Motivated by this inner urge we talk about God. I have told you all about God. No, this is not a fact. Nobody has been able to have the last word on God so far. This is our feeling. But in Christianity and in Islam whatever is said is supposed to be the last word. In Hinduism no one can have the last word on God. It is not at all possible to pass the final verdict on God.

Energy fields
Now I would like to say a few words on the energy that is generated by this yajna. A hotel has an atmosphere of its own. Every place has its own environment; you can call it an atmosphere. Scholars and scientists have said that human

87

beings breathe in oxygen and breathe out carbon. In the same manner they emit thought waves, they emit positive and negative energy. Energy is generated within us and its quantum increases and decreases, expands and contracts. This is called the energy field. People say they can feel low energy or negative energy at a particular place. We say there is a great energy field here.

What is energy? Is it a vibration? Is it a temperature? Mantras are very powerful means of generating an energy field. Pooja also has great potency in generating an energy field. You may perform the pooja here or in your home. In India the pooja is held in a *thakur bari*, a small place of worship. Energy of different kinds is generated there. Feelings of pain and pleasure, honour and dishonour, hope and despair, profit and loss, all generate energy. This energy confuses us, we are dazed, we go insane, we become worried. We have different kinds of feelings. We get sick, we become perturbed, we take drugs, we fight, we take to drink, we smoke and so on. Why? Because the energy being generated in our surroundings is closely related to our life pattern. Our life pattern changes from age to age. For the last fifty years the life pattern has undergone a sea change. We are producing confusing energy and so at times even well balanced people become confused.

Resolve of surrender

Now the Devi recitation is over. This year's resolve is: "O Mother, may our actions benefit others and ourselves so that when we leave this body it is with a smile. Give us such wisdom as may remove the darkness from our lives. We are ignorant and incapacitated. We are incapable of warding off ill will and follies. Now you alone will save us from falling into the abyss." This is a resolve of total surrender. Singing in praise of God, worshipping God with full devotion, is a great thing. Now Swami Niranjan will sing the chorus and we will repeat it. This is our resolve for this year.

Swami Niranjan: Sri Swamiji has selected this song to express this year's resolve because the whole of humanity is agitated

88

and perturbed. Humankind is being terrorized. Everyone is confounded and bewildered by the circumstances around us. There is tension and violence all over the world. Darkness prevails and no one knows in which direction to move. People have lost their inner strength. Once you lose faith, confidence and reverence, you are left with nothing to depend on. They are life's precious possessions and you cling to them when faced with a crisis. *Shraddha* and *vishwas,* reverence and faith, have been the main planks of life from time immemorial. As stated in the opening lines of the *Ramacharitamanas,*

Bhavaanishankarau vande shraddhaavishwaasarupinau
Yaabhyaamvinaa na pashyaanti siddhaah svaantahsthameeshwaram.

"Shiva and his consort Parvati are the embodiments of reverence and faith, without which even the adept cannot achieve spiritual attainment."

Faith and reverence are the precious possessions of life; they represent the inner prosperity of human life. Prosperity relates to your mental affluence, not your worldly wealth. When your mind is full of faith and reverence and when this flows towards God and is reflected in your day-to-day actions and deeds, then your life is filled with peace and happiness. This peace and happiness does not remain confined to one's personal life, but permeates the whole family. The total environment is surcharged. Physical and mental diseases disappear. This is the impact of this resolve. Sri Swamiji has chosen this song at the time of Devi worship so that we may connect with inner faith and reverence.

The song is known and sung all over India. Join us in the singing with verve and enthusiasm. Sing it not only here but wherever you go, even in your home. But do not sing it like a film song. Put your heart and soul into it and sing with full devotion so that it may connect you with God.

Satsang 9

December 16, 2001, Morning

Today is the second day of the yajna and we will complete the offering of gifts to the local villagers. Over a thousand families from five villages are participating. With the first chanting of the mantra, we will start distributing prasad to them. The people sitting in front of me come from the villages in my circle, which has a population of about ten thousand. It is called Rikhia panchayat. When I came here in 1989 these people were living like orphans. My arrival has made a substantial change to their destiny. I compelled the electricity department to install transformers so they now receive electricity. Many other activities are taking place, such as education. The boys and girls all go to school. Tomorrow you will see the girls from this area who go to Deoghar for higher education. We provide them with bicycles so they can travel independently and safely.

When you extend your hand in friendship I become your friend. When you wish to be my companion I follow suit. This means either you have compelled me or I have compelled you. We have compelled each other. Friendship or comradeship is a great victory. Friendship is the most powerful weapon of mankind. The promotion of friendliness is great politics. Are you listening? The attainment of friendship is great politics.

Sri Swamiji, 2001

Swami Niranjan, 2001

Sri Swamiji during the Rasalila, 2001

Engrossed in the Rasalila

Enjoying the program

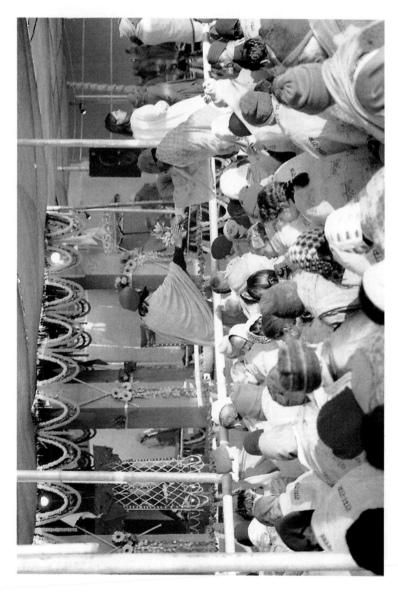

Yajnashala

Chanting Durga Saptashati

Prasad Distribution

Sri Swamiji with sannyasins and devotees

Devi, 2001

Swami Niranjan fulfilling a duty during the Rajasooya Yajna

Load bearers of society

The villagers are very simple people; they are the load bearers of our society. Do you know what load bearers are? In a building, the columns, beams and foundations bear the load of the house, not the windows, furniture or decorations. People like us are the interior decoration. They are the load bearers of our society and once they crack society will break. Therefore, it is very important that we recognize their role in society and also accept their existence as a reality. They are very mobile people, very strong people. They are the weight bearers of our society. Just as beams and columns bear the load of a building similarly the common folk in any country – the labourers, taxi drivers, rickshaw pullers and thela pullers – are the load bearers of society. If this society cracks and breaks, then there will be chaos.

Therefore, it becomes our duty, your duty, everyone's duty, to sustain this society. Only if the columns of the building are strong will they bear the weight of the house, otherwise the building will collapse. Society will collapse. Society does not depend on us. We are the load, we are not the load-bearers. People like us are a burden on society; we are not the bearers of the burden. Therefore, it is our duty in every society – Eastern or Western, African, Chinese or Russian – to care for the common folk, because their needs are very few. What they consume in one year, an American or European consumes in one second. I am talking about their consumption of oxygen, food and water. So you can understand how economical they are for your existence, for your society. We have to learn this lesson.

I am very glad that today the villagers will be receiving prasad. They have been receiving prasad since I came here, but this time I wanted to tell all of you that you have a duty, a compulsory obligation. In every society not only in India, there are common people who tend cows, take care of sheep, drive taxis and do all kinds of other jobs like plumbing and electricity. They are the supports of your society. When society breaks, anarchy takes place. Anarchy does not take place because there is a lot wrong with us. If we are destroyed, nothing will happen. But if their society is destroyed the country will go to the dogs. It has always happened in history and that is why we Indians are very careful about it. Everywhere in India they are invited to yajnas.

Play of give and take

The monsoon rises from the sea and finally settles. If the sea did not allow the monsoon to emerge, there would be no rain and if there were no rain, there would be no monsoon. So there is a play of give and take. One who gives receives the same thing back. In yajna the same thing happens. It is said that in ancient times King Harshavardhana gave away all his personal property at the conclusion of performing the Rajasooya Yajna. It is an historical fact, not a myth. He had attended the Maha Kumbha at Prayag. There he gifted away all his personal possessions and thereafter ate his meals from leaf plates, drank water from an earthen pot and slept on the bare ground. Think of it, the Emperor of Hindustan donated everything that he possessed and slept on the ground! He did that because offering is one of the three components of yajna. This is a part of the Indian tradition. Sri Rama also performed the Rajasooya Yajna as well as many other sacrifices. Our yajna concludes in twelve years. The first year is a rehearsal.

Foundation of the nation

I want to emphasize the point that the general populace are the load bearers of society. They are the foundation of the nation. The king is not the cornerstone of the country or the nation. It is the subjects, the masses, that provide the base, the solid ground, the direction, the destination for a nation to move forward, not the king or the ruler. The king cannot build the nation; it is the masses who build the nation. The ruler is just our representative. He cannot be our master. The rulers are our servants. The subjects are above the king. It is the nation builders, the masses, that constitute society. Intellectuals and their ideologies are numbered. Newspapers and magazines highlight their activities and it appears that they constitute the core of society, but they do not represent the philosophy of the masses.

The national philosophy of India will be determined by that sixty percent of the population. The cultivators, the labourers, the downtrodden and the destitute constitute the mass of the Indian population and they will determine the philosophy. You all belong to that class. There was a time when your forefathers used to live in huts and thatched houses and draw water from wells. Your grandmothers used to go out to relieve themselves before sunrise with a tin of water. You have forgotten that because you have stepped into a different culture. Please don't forget this is an artificial culture, it is a temporary phase. Real culture is independent and long lasting. No one can prevent us from going to the forest with a tin pot. The jungle is there, the tin pot is there and the water pool is there; they can be used without interference from any quarter. All these things exist without government intervention.

Independent culture

What do the women of this area do early in the morning? During autumn when the trees lose their leaves, they stir from their homes and collect the fallen dry leaves, sweeping them up with their brooms and stacking them inside their houses. They don't have to go to the market to purchase fire wood or gas cylinders. Some of you may not be aware how independent they are. They use these dry leaves as firewood and cook their daily food in a small cooking pot. They don't need much. It makes no difference to them whether there is a government or not. The dry leaves, the cooking pot, the fire and one's stomach are all there. No social or governmental intervention is required. This is an independent culture. They draw water for cooking and drinking purposes from the village tank. They go to the fields to relieve themselves and their ablutions are finished by sunrise. Thus they lead a spartan life independent of external aids.

This kind of culture is not dependent on a king, on wealth or on any other resources. It depends on no external resources. If there is no government or king, I can survive on my own. To inculcate this kind of culture we sannyasins are given training of this type while we are in our guru's ashram. We have slept without a roof and bathed in the Ganga in the shivering cold of winter too. If you can't afford a dhoti make do with a loin cloth. Many sadhus declare that they don't even need a loin cloth! Lie down somewhere in a corner. Self-imposed discipline is a very important component of a society and a culture.

Self-imposed poverty is a way of life that is independent of the external world. Even if you are millionaire or a multimillionaire, try to skip one meal one day. If you go to a pilgrimage centre, lie down on the bare earth for a day. One should try to be independent. When I meet these people, I often say, "With a push cart you are independent. You earn sixty rupees a day and live an honest life. You need not earn six hundred rupees a day and be dishonest!"

Learning the habit of giving

For a human being, the most difficult vow is to forsake, to renounce, to let go. Everyone knows how to collect, how to add up. Every child learns this art in his mother's womb, but you require a guru to learn how to let go or renounce. To renounce means to make a sacrifice. Sacrifice is made for the sake of others, just as a mother makes sacrifices and abstains from many comforts for the sake of her child's well-being. A time should come in this country, in this land of the Ganga, Yamuna and Saraswati, when people cultivate the habit of giving. Everyone should inculcate the attitude of giving. You should give to everyone, even the affluent, not only to the poor and the destitute. God does not discriminate between rich and poor. He gives to all. He gives to the poorest of the poor and the wealthiest of the wealthy too. He gives to the Tatas, the Birlas and the Ambanis as well as to the beggars. If you go to the lanes and alleys of Varanasi, you will find a host of beggars and they too are treated well. This is the way of God and we should learn it.

Local villagers

All the people sitting here are connected with this institution in one way or another. They are from the nearby villages of Lodhia, Pairhidih and Rudrapur. I have to throw some light on these villagers. When I came to Rikhia in 1989 there was nothing in this area, it was a desolate place. People living in my neighbourhood had no hope for the future. Now this area is humming with life. Activities are going on round the clock. My neighbours have done a lot to improve this area. They have installed all the structures you see here: the canopies, the pandals, the pavilion. Our sannyasins have put up the barricading, however, because sannyasins have to be karma yogis as well as raja yogis and jnana yogis.

I did not hire any artisans or mechanics from Kanpur, Calcutta, Delhi or Mumbai. There has been no contract work. We have engaged local labourers. My neighbours have done everything – digging excavations, installing pipes, erecting canopies. They have done the bricklaying, electrical fittings and plumbing and set up the transformers you see on the premises. They have also set up the sewage system, and you will not find such an efficient system even in Delhi!

Some of these villagers are cultivators, others are labourers, push carters, rickshaw pullers and porters. Quite a few own tempos and trekkers, which are their means of livelihood. Some are toddy tappers; they take out juice from the toddy trees. A number of people drink toddy. The world cannot be free of toddy takers. God has created a strange world which consists of many types of people. He has created many obstructions too on the way to moksha. He probably thought that if all living beings became liberated, then who would worship God? People remember God and recount His virtues only when they are in distress and when they are out of the woods they forget God. So God devised a plan to put people in distress and misery so that they may remember Him and recount His virtues. When there is no pain and distress, then what is the role of God? I have just told you all this by way of a joke. I don't know how far it is from the truth. It is up to you to judge what the truth is.

Some of these villagers were not born when I came here in 1989. The twelve-year-old boys and girls have no knowledge of my arrival. Some of the girls I have selected for Kanya pooja are quite new to this place. Some of the young women working as labourers know nothing about pregnancy or labour pain. When they complain that something is jumping inside their womb, little do they realize what it is. When unknowingly they complain of labour pain we get an ambulance immediately to take them to the maternity centre.

Formative years

I also come from the same class and I am aware of the problems you face in your day-to-day lives. For twenty years I was a farmer's son. My family had fifteen hundred acres of land plus one thousand acres of forest acquired through a deed of gift. We had no right to dispose of it according to the land laws prevalent in the Kumaon division of Uttar Pradesh. The ownership and the title of the property went to the eldest son. The property could not be divided. So we were cultivators.

On weekdays we would go to town to pursue our studies. We had a small house in the town also. On Saturday we would return to our village by pony and stay at home on Saturday and Sunday to look after the domestic work. We had a large number of oxen and cows and five hundred sheep from which we procured wool. The sheep used to roam freely in the forest. Besides this we had twelve large dogs, which we had purchased from Tibet. These dogs took care of the sheep in the forest and protected them from fierce animals. The forests were very dense and infested with lions and tigers. I used to wander about in the forest and enjoy the forest life.

When I came home on holidays, I would play sport. I was fond of cricket, but I hardly ever played cricket because it is a whole day affair and took up too much time. I was a farmer's son and if I wasted my whole day playing cricket, then who would supervise the domestic work? Cricket is the passion of those who have too much money. It is a luxury. Football is the ideal game for India. You finish the game in one hour and can then attend to your domestic work. Who can afford to play for the whole day? Only those with money, who do not have to go out and earn a living. Only the white collared babus can afford to do it.

Guru's ashram

I wish to emphasize that I too come from the same class as the villagers. For twenty years I also used to go to the fields with a tin pot. Then I spent twelve years in my guru's ashram and I led a much harder life there. In the ashram I had no place of my own to sleep. I had no plate. I had to beg in the villages for rotis to eat. There was no money to purchase food. The only mission was to serve my guru, and this service to Guruji opened the doors to my fortune.

Whatever I had learnt at school was of no use in the ashram. I did not remember the names of Aurangzeb's or Akbar's wives and sons. Suddenly the names of Shankaracharya, Lord Buddha, Mahavir, Tulsidas, Kabirdas, Surdas, Meera, Keshavdas and other saints and ascetics flashed into my mind. I forgot Akbar, Jehangir and Aurangzeb and Noor Jehan. These names will not serve any purpose for you either. Even if you have committed them to memory, it won't help you in life. The sayings of sadhus and mahatmas may help you. The words and discourses of scholarly and saintly persons like Meera, Tulsidas and Shankaracharya will come to your rescue. The sayings of Lord Krishna in the *Bhagavad Gita* will help you to fashion your life. These things helped me a great deal to work out the course of my life.

During my twelve year sojourn in my guru's ashram, I toiled very hard. I worked so hard that my bones were visible and could be counted. I became so lean and thin that people used to ask if I ever got anything to eat in the ashram. One gentleman asked, "What kind of brahmachari are you? All your bones are visible?" He thought that a brahmachari should look plump. I retorted, "No, a brahmachari should not be plump; he should be light and slim, not pot-bellied!"

97

As Yogi Gorakhnath has said in *Gorakh Vani*, "If a disciple is fat and flabby, it means he has not encountered the right guru."

Parivrajaka

After leaving my guru's ashram I spent some time in Varanasi where I followed the routine of the beggars. Every day in the early morning I used to squat at the Dashashwamedha Ghat in line with the beggars with my scarf spread out in my lap. This was in 1956, nearly fifty years ago, when many of you were not born. I used to get five rupees as alms every day and with this earning I ate puri-kachori in the evening and slept somewhere in Kabir Chaura, wherever I could find a space.

I spent twenty years in my village home as a farmer's son and twelve years in my guru's ashram without rest or comfort. After leaving Rishikesh I again spent another twelve years as a wandering sannyasin. So, after forty-four years I landed at Munger in Bihar.

Divine gift

God told me, "Swami Satyananda, as long as you are not amassing wealth for your own comfort and luxury you will get whatever you want." Mother Lakshmi has issued a blank cheque, but it is not meant for my personal comfort. Be it the earthquake in Bhuj or the Orissa catastrophe, I can spend as much as I like on relief measures for disaster affected people. That divine gift is always there for me. It is a service to the nation.

I wish to emphasize one point. The tendency to collect and amass property gives rise to wrong conduct; it leads to undesirable thought processes and unholy attitudes. However, the tendency to sacrifice brings about a complete change in man's behaviour, his way of thinking, his way of living, his way of expression. This is the statement of our sages and seers. If you fill a bottle with water and do not use it, the water putrefies. If the water continues to flow, it never putrefies. This should be the attitude of human behaviour.

Service not moksha

Saints are born to help others, to serve others. Saints and ascetics are not born to seek their own liberation; it is not their mission. Householders seek moksha, worldly people seek liberation or final salvation because they are miserable. One who is in bondage needs release. One who feels he is a prisoner wants to be set free. If you feel that this world is a veritable bondage, only then will you seek release from this bondage. If you do so you must get it.

But why should I seek liberation? I fail to understand what will I do in the next world. I may be happy in the next world too where I will serve God. I am also quite at home in Rikhia. If I have to shift somewhere else tomorrow I will be happy there. I remain happy in every situation, in every country, in every association, in every garb, in every hue and colour, in every circumstance. I adjust myself to every mode and method. Saints and seers never seek final liberation; they do not need it. Only those need moksha who are in chains, in bondage, who are miserable, who are in terrible agony, who are frustrated and worried. One who is sick needs a doctor.

Does a river drink its own water? Do fruits and vegetables such as mangoes, guavas, apples, papaya, jack fruit, tomatoes or potatoes eat themselves? No, they are for all of us. This is called *paramartha*, the highest service. That which helps others is paramartha and that which is of no help to others is selfishness. Man's greatest weakness is miserliness. Devas run after enjoyment, demons are cruel and human beings are miserly. So devas have to be learn self-restraint, demons have to learn to be kind and human beings have to learn to give.

Satsang 10

December 16, 2001, Afternoon

Swami Niranjan: Yajnas have a very special meaning because they invoke the divine spirit and create a spiritual atmosphere. However, the yajna being conducted here at Rikhia Dham takes on a different meaning because it is not like a fair where people come and go and witness the proceedings, spend ten minutes or half an hour and then walk out. People come here to imbibe the spiritual energy which permeates the environment and atmosphere. When they become one with that atmosphere and energy, then that energy creates a subtle transformation and fulfils the purpose of the yajna.

Our mind is made up of habits, thoughts, desires and so on. We have emotions and feelings which we express from time to time in different ways. We have intuition and wisdom which comes to the surface from time to time, otherwise our mind is clouded by the negative and destructive tendencies which permeate our environment. When we come to the yajna with that ordinary mind, it undergoes a subtle transformation which cannot be analyzed rationally by the intellect. That change takes place just by being in the presence of the yajna. When you go swimming, the water covers the entire body. Similarly, when you are in an atmosphere where such auspicious activities are taking place, the psyche is surrounded by the vibration and the yajna evokes and creates a change in the perception of the human psyche.

Threefold purpose of yajna

Sri Swamiji has said many times that yajna has a threefold purpose. The first purpose is production, *utpadana;* this is also the meaning of 'ya', the first syllable of the word yajna. The second purpose of yajna is distribution, *vikara*, and the third is assimilation, *bhoga*. These are the three events that take place in a yajna. The tradition, the scriptures, the saints have all spoken of yajna as a process that governs the whole of creation, the whole of life. The food that you cook in your kitchen is yajna – you are producing food. The same meal that you distribute to your family fulfils the second purpose of yajna – you are distributing food. Eating, assimilation, consumption, fulfils the third purpose of yajna. So, even the acts that are performed naturally from the time of birth to death are yajna. Even the education you receive in a gurukul, a school, a college or a university is yajna. These three processes happen naturally within you without any effort.

Of course, the difference is that your awareness is not there. Without awareness it is just a routine activity. Yoga has always said, "Maintain awareness of the present and in that way you can become a yogi." Saints have said, "Maintain awareness of the present and in that way you can become a better person." Unfortunately, however, human beings tend to live in the past, ignore the present and remain fearful of the future. That is not the concept of humanism, as described in the ancient tradition, that is alive today. It is this shift in consciousness which has to take place.

From being fearful of the future, we develop clarity, a clear vision of the future. That clear vision is also attained by becoming aware of the process of life as yajna. From ignoring the present, we become aware of the needs of the present and how we can improve the situation and the environment to make it more fulfilling for each and every individual, recognizing that God permeates, lives and exists in everything.

101

Om ishaavaasyamidam sarvam yatkincha jagatyaam jagat,
tena tyaktena bhunjeethaa maa gridhah kasyasvid dhanam.

"All that exists in this ever-changing universe is the abode of the Lord (in which the Lord resides). Enjoy whatever the Lord gives you. Do not covet, for whose indeed is wealth?"

This is the statement of the fortieth chapter of the *Yajur Veda*, the first mantra of the *Ishavasya Upanishad*. Similarly this is the concept, the vision, the idea which develops in spiritual life. Yajna is a part of that spirituality inherent in every being. It is not a fire ceremony, that is one aspect. It is not recitation of mantras, that is one aspect. It is not invocation of the higher forces, that is one aspect. That is the ritualistic aspect, known as *karmakanda*. When that external ritual becomes internal, that is known as *upasana*, and when that internal ritual becomes a part of your expression in life, that is known as yajna.

Head, heart and hands

This yajna is a combination not only of knowledge but also of faith, belief and action. Swami Sivananda used to say that in order to experience completeness in life one should combine jnana, karma and bhakti. Sri Swamiji has said many times that a human being is composed of the three qualities of head, heart and hands. Head represents the intellect, *jnana*; heart represents the *bhavana*, the feeling, the sentiment, the emotion; and hands represents action, performance, participation. People suffer when they ignore one of these aspects of life. Tension, frustration and a destructive environment in society are the outcome of ignoring a function and a quality of life which one can attain.

Yajna is a complete process of living that spiritual life, not only at a personal level, not only at a social level but also at an ecological level. In the past, yajna had an impact on ecology, both human ecology and global ecology. That impact is a very powerful one. We hear and read about homes from which the smoke and fire of the yajna would emanate three times a day, morning, afternoon and evening. The smoke from the yajna would purify not only the atmosphere of the house but also the global atmosphere, removing not only the external pollution but also the mental pollution.

Mental pollution is a very great disease that we all have. Cancer can be managed but not mental constipation. AIDS can be managed but not mental diarrhoea. Mental and emotional diarrhoea are the results of a disturbed mind, an unbalanced mind, a destructive mind, a mind that is not still. It is that environment which changes when you become part of the process of yajna and when yajna manifests in your life as belief, action and lifestyle. That is true yoga. Hatha yoga is good for the body; it can remove your constipation and provide you with better health. Raja yoga is good for the mind; it can help to still the agitated mind temporarily and it can help you change certain habits. Bhakti yoga is good for channelling the emotions. But all these yogas are integrated in this process of yajna, where you begin to perceive yourself as the offerer and the offering. Your actions become the offering. This is what the sages and saints in the past have taught all of us.

Becoming free
During this yajna the external aspect is learning how to give. You have heard Sri Swamiji say many times that we are all selfish people. We like to accumulate things. For whom? We don't know. We collect for our pleasure but does it really give us pleasure? Accumulation brings more headaches. You can live with one pair of shoes, but you accumulate twenty pairs because each new pair looks nicer than the last. You don't even wear them once a month and your house becomes a museum due to accumulation. What mentality does that represent? A mentality that does not know how to give, but only how to accumulate, an accumulation that has no purpose.

The external aspect and the major aspect of the yajna is learning how to give, how to let go of your attachments to what you accumulate. Once we are able to do that we become free spiritually, we become free as human beings. That freedom is defined in many ways. For a sannyasin that freedom is defined in karma. For a *grihastha*, a householder, that freedom is defined in *aradhana*, worship. For a *tyagi*, a renunciate, that freedom is defined in letting go of all attachments. The important point is that you become free, and it is that freedom that we seek in our life.

Krishna and Shishupala

Sri Swamiji: The Rajasooya Yajna was performed during the time of Lord Rama and Lord Krishna. When the Emperor Yudhishthira performed this yajna, do you know which duty Lord Krishna had? He did not serve food. The duty he assigned himself was washing the feet of the guests and removing and disposing of their leaf plates after the feast. That Sudarshandhari god, who was an incarnation of the Almighty, washed the feet of the guests and removed their plates after they had finished eating!

Shishupala, the son of Lord Krishna's maternal aunt, abused Lord Krishna publicly in front of all those assembled for the Rajasooya Yajna, calling him a thief, a villain, an adulterer. But Lord Krishna tolerated Shishupala and remained silent. When his followers asked him why he was silent, he replied that he had promised Shishupala's mother he would spare him as long as he had not committed one hundred sins. When Shishupala cursed Lord Krishna for the ninety-ninth time, the Lord cautioned him, saying, "Shishupala, just one remains. You can stop and be spared the wrath of the Lord." But the foolish Shishupala continued to abuse Lord Krishna and as soon as he had finished uttering the hundredth curse, Krishna threw the Sudarshan chakra, severing Shishupala's neck from his body.

This is a story from one Rajasooya Yajna. But don't be afraid that we will do that here! The times have changed. My parents and grandparents advised me to win over the world by virtue of the teachings of the shastras because the age of the sword is over. Now, in Kali Yuga, one has to conquer the world through the power of scriptural knowledge, through humility, not with pride and force. So,

104

I am not going to use the Sudarshan chakra. I have only one way of changing the world, which is turning the other cheek. Animosity cannot be quelled with animosity. The sword cannot silence the sword; the sword is silenced by love. This is the teaching of the saints and sages.

Laksha Chandi Yajna

Today the pooja is being performed with almonds, tomorrow with red flowers, the day after with roses and on the last day with lotuses. The worship will be done on different days with different flowers. Whenever you find time, do not hesitate to do *pradakshina*, circumambulation of Devi. The chanting of *Durga Saptashati* is now half finished, so the major part of this yajna is also over.

After the pooja, the *Sankalpa Gita*, the song of resolve, will be sung. Arati will follow and then prasad will be distributed. Come prepared tomorrow to sit and observe the proceedings from seven to ten, from eleven to one and from two to five. So tomorrow is a very big program. Prasad will be offered to those who have come from abroad. We have here today people from Iran and I have full faith that in a few years from now yoga aspirants from Afghanistan will also be coming.

This year fewer people from abroad have come because of the events of last September in America. The number of visitors has dropped because the number of flights has been reduced, especially from Europe. Still many countries are represented here. Next year the number of participants should double. Hence, although we have embarked upon Sat Chandi Yajna, which is one hundred recitations, it has turned into Laksha Chandi Yajna, one hundred thousand recitations, in view of the chanting by thousands of aspirants. If hundreds of people chant together and if you calculate on that basis, then the sum total of recitations will exceed a *lakh*, which is one hundred thousand.

Prayer to God

Swami Niranjan: "*Ai malik tere bande ham*" is the greatest and most sublime prayer to the Mother Goddess. The underlying resolve is that our deeds should be such that we walk the path of goodness and withdraw from ill deeds so that we can depart this earth with a smile on our faces. Our seers have always said and Indian culture always prescribes that we must acquire pious thoughts, behave properly and perform good deeds, and that is the desired religion of humanity. Hypocrisy and blind faith cannot guide us nor can they be followed as true religions. There are certain faiths and beliefs on which one can concentrate for a period, but ultimately that must culminate only in right and good deeds. Such belief or faith must be reflected in your *achara*, conduct, *vichara*, thoughts, and *vyavahara*, deeds. Nobody becomes righteous simply by wearing the garb of a Hindu, a Christian, a Muslim, a Sikh, a Jain or a Buddhist. A human being cannot be called righteous simply by following a particular sect or the prayers of a certain religion. One is truly religious or righteous only when this is reflected in one's conduct, thoughts and actions

Indian culture has defined our religion in the same way, often called noble thoughts, behaviour and deeds. One attains these qualities through a dedicated resolve in which one prays to God for such noble thoughts, behaviour and deeds. We sing this in our song of resolve, which is sung here as a prayer. You may also sing this song in your homes to derive inspiration. This is not just a film song. It is the inner outburst of the noble feelings of those who can see only darkness and despondency on all sides. When the environment becomes fearful and there is no other source of strength, only then does such an outburst pour from within, from the inner self. In reality then this is the real prayer of a devotee to God.

Prasad

Sri Swamiji: You must all take your prasad at the gate. We will meet again tomorrow. When the yajna of the Mother Goddess concludes and you all return home, we will again be offering Devi's prasad to your family members and neighbours. This year we have had three lakhs, three hundred thousand, laddoos prepared for everybody. My old friends, their children, their children's children number in the thousands and they have to be offered prasad. I am not a young man. I have been making friends for the last sixty or seventy years and the number is increasing day by day. I shall give them all laddoos as prasad.

Satsang 11

December 17, 2001, Morning

*T*oday is the third day of the yajna and prasad will be distributed to approximately nine hundred children from the middle schools. Oh, what a sight it will be! The whole area will be teeming with children. Every year we give them school bags, reading, writing and painting materials, notebooks, coloured pencils, pastels, erasers, pencil sharpeners, instrument boxes, games and toys, everything they will need for one year of study, including school uniforms. Once the local education officer was passing by one of his own government schools and he was surprised to find all the boys and girls in uniform. When he enquired from the teachers whether it was a new Christian missionary school, he was flabbergasted to learn that it was one of his own government schools. He was very happy because no government school provides uniforms for the children. He came and thanked me.

When I first arrived in Rikhia neither the children nor their parents showed any interest in their studies. I was surprised because my feeling was that if the sannyasins in the ashram are so highly educated, then householders and their children should also be knowledgeable. We have arranged classes for teaching English, which start from Makar Sankranti, January the fourteenth. People from Patna,

Bangalore and other places come and spend their time teaching these students, who are very small children from the surrounding villages. Almost all the children come from labourers' families, where the breadwinner pulls a rickshaw or a thela, or is a coolie, or a ploughman or weaves mats. They have developed a great interest in their education.

Importance of education

The local girls attend classes here in the ashram for six months a year. The multiplication tables are all spoken in English. They don't say, "Do ekam do, do dooni chaar, do tiya chhah," they say, "Two ones are two, two twos are four, two threes are six" and so on. All the students read in English. They not only read English but practise it too. Whenever I come across them during my morning stroll, they say, "Good morning, Swamiji," and also enquire, "How are you?" When I ask how they are, they say, "Fine." We should not decide what the language of our country should be. It should be decided by the labourers because a labourer is pragmatic, he is practical. He is close to reality. So these children now speak English. They also sing English songs. The day is not far off when they will sing pop songs too, and this pop music has a very good rhythm. In music the metre should be correct like our kirtans, which are so good. Haven't you seen us singing kirtan with the right timing and rhythm?

When the girls saw Swami Satsangi speaking English so fluently, they were surprised. They were even more astonished when they saw her driving vehicles. So they followed suit and the process of education among the girls began. The girls of this area now go to Deoghar, eight kilometres away, on bicycles, which have been provided by this ashram. In my opinion, education in this age is tantamount to having the third eye, *jnana chakshu*. No society can prosper without that education. Without education a society cannot march forward.

These children have developed an intense interest in their studies and their education. We give them all the books they require. For girls, we have arranged music and singing

109

classes. There is a big classroom for them here and they now sing that English song, "Come here, my dear, Krishna Kanhai." We have put up educational charts for them. Today is their day. Their parents and other family members have already received their prasad. Today we will offer the children what they deserve.

In the afternoon, the grown up girls of this panchayat who are not yet married will be given prasad separately again. All the other girls have received something. Only these grown up girls have been left out and surely if they are not given something they will complain that when the whole of society runs after them, Swamiji has ignored them. So, I have decided to present them with something too.

Take care of your society

These children and their parents are the load bearers of our society, like the beams and columns of a house. If the column and beam are weak, the society will collapse, as is happening in Afghanistan, in Kosovo, in Africa and many other countries. This section of society must be looked after properly. If it is not looked after properly, then there will be rape, there will be looting, there will be extremism, there will be terrorism. Then you will never be safe. The government cannot give you protection, the army, the military, cannot give you protection. No government can protect its citizens if this section of the population is ignored. This section comprises sixty to seventy percent of India and also of the whole world.

Why is extremism taking place? Why is terrorism taking place? Because this section is deprived and ignored. Money is spent in cities. These people have no education, no drinking water, no facilities for irrigation and you are building sports stadiums worth millions of rupees. Why? In order to tell people, "Look, we have nice stadiums is this country." If I do not look after the children from this section of society, my ashram will not be safe. Society cannot be given security if the larger section of the country is not looked after. Practically sixty to seventy percent of the world's population is neglected. I am not just talking about India. Anywhere in Africa, even in China, even in Russia, they are not looked after. When I came to Rikhia, this was the first thing God told me. He said, "If you want blessings help the people and the blessings are open to you. Help the people and all doors are open to you. If you need money help people. I'll give you a blank cheque."

This is a message to each and everyone in this country. If you bake four loaves of bread, one loaf is for society. You have to share your joy, your booty, your money. You have to share your happiness with everyone. You don't have to give charity indiscriminately. Nor am I hinting that you should give me the money. I don't need your money at all! Most ashrams thrive on donations from disciples, but the Bihar School of Yoga in Munger and Sivananda Math do not need or depend on your money. This is a very frank and challenging reply that I give to people.

So, please do not misunderstand me when I call upon you to take care of the society in which you live and prosper. My philosophy is simple and straight. It has been repeated by our spiritual leaders from time immemorial. Everyone should ponder over the plight of that section of society which has been kept deprived for so long. The main cause of extremism in most countries is because the majority of a section of society has been neglected and kept deprived of the basic minimum needs. What does the government do? Nothing. It only passes bills in parliament. No child receives the things they need to learn to read and write with. In this area I provide the students with these things. Did you know that one notebook costs up to twenty rupees. We give twelve to fourteen notebooks to each student. We give pencils which someone sends from Japan. Someone else sends stationery items from England.

Equal rights for women
We also give bicycles to those girls who go to school in Deoghar. I help the girls because we have to atone for all the oppression heaped upon girls and women in the past. This

111

is an obligation we have to fulfil. Women have been tortured and are being humiliated even today in India. Their rights and privileges have been snatched away. Many degrading rules have been imposed on them. All the facilities and privileges centre only around men. Women and girls are ordered not to do this and not to do that. Widows are forced to wear white clothes. Does a widower do the same? Widows are forced to shave their heads. Why aren't widowers also compelled to do that? All these rules of society are for women only. Widows cannot even wear a ring! So, I directed that all the widows of this panchayat should be offered coloured saris. India and Indians have to atone for the heartless acts and atrocities committed towards women.

The truth is that men and women must have equal rights. The rules governing both must be the same. The civil and social laws must be similar; they cannot and should not be unequal and different. The same laws should apply to both men and women. Why can't a girl go somewhere alone like a boy does? Only because some of the boys may get up to mischief with her. If a girl is made stronger and more confident from the very beginning, then if anyone tries to misbehave with her she will slap his face. Girls should be allowed to grow strong from early childhood and must not be kept under restraint. In Europe and America, if a boy tries to take liberties with a girl she immediately says, "Sorry," and the boy can't take any liberties. Some of the girls who are bold enough use their sandals to defend themselves, which is not a remedy.

Education and profession before marriage

These girls should be properly educated and trained. You must all study hard. In the past girls had only one future, which was to get married and produce children. Now they have a future on many fronts. They can study, acquire knowledge and obtain a degree – BA, MA, LLB, BCom, MCom, BSc, MSc, become doctors, engineers, learn about computers and electronics, be well versed in biotechnology, and so on. Then they can find a job and stand on their own two feet. They can hold a job in a bank, in schools and colleges, become doctors or lawyers, a collector or a super-intendent of police. After they have done that, then they can marry. There is no harm in marrying. I never prohibit marriage, but I must reiterate that marriage is not the only future for a girl. A hundred years ago marriage might have been a proposition, but now their future lies in higher education.

A girl has to marry and the matter is decided by her parents. I fail to understand this thinking. If I have to marry, the choice of boy or girl should be my prerogative. How can it be my marriage and your choice? In the next five, ten or fifteen years the times will change and a girl will be bold enough to say, "If the boy you have selected for me is so virtuous and accomplished, why don't you marry him? If it is up to me, I will marry the boy of my choice, one whose parents will not demand a dowry. I earn ten thousand rupees a month, which comes to one hundred and twenty thousand rupees per annum. Tell me, why should the boy's parents demand a dowry?"

The boy or his parents who demand a dowry from the parents of a girl who is fully employed are downright fools. Lawyers and doctors earn a decent salary. The minimum monthly salary of a doctor may be thirty thousand rupees and if a lady doctor earns thirty thousand rupees per month her annual earnings would be three hundred and sixty thousand rupees. The society that demands a dowry from such a girl is a fool. If you want to make progress, you have to keep in mind the reasons why society is moving in the wrong direction. Otherwise go on treading the beaten path, wearing a red trade mark on your forehead and covered from head to foot in a red sari. Be prepared to be beaten up by your drunken husband, to lie down in a corner of the house and also to go on reproducing indiscriminately.

Treasure of learning
This will not happen in the future. The children here are learning to read and write in the schools. Go on pursuing

your studies sincerely and become self-reliant. Today you will all receive prasad. There are notebooks in your schoolbag, a geometry set, pens and pencils. Your bag also contains a T-shirt and trousers, and one invisible thing – my feelings and blessings. You may not see that but the feeling of my heart is there.

In the twentieth sloka of *Neetishatak*, Bhartrihari states,

Vidyanaam narasye roopamadhikam prachchhahnaguptam dhanam
Vidya bhogkari yashah sukhakari vidya gurunam guruh.
Vidya bandhujano videshgamane
Vidya paramdaivatam.

"Learning is man's abundant beauty, it is his hidden treasure. Learning is a source of enjoyment, fame and pleasure, learning is the super preceptor. While in a foreign country learning is your friend and guide. Learning is supreme fortune."

I have travelled in foreign countries. Swami Vivekananda travelled in foreign countries. We won the world by dint of our learning and knowledge. Learning, knowledge and wisdom are required to win the world. Therefore, you should take a keen interest in your studies and acquire knowledge to stand on your own feet. You should motivate your parents also to learn something. Devote more time to your studies.

Education comes first

I have to give the same message to the boys also. Avoid idle rambling, avoid the company of cigarette smokers, tobacco chewers and those youngsters who are fond of liquor. Maintain a respectful distance from those idlers who have no stake in life. If you have to fashion a decent future, you should take your career seriously. I am particularly addressing the young boys. The government has offered a number of concessions to the backward classes. You must try to avail yourselves of these concessions without resorting to underhand methods.

I give books and stationery to a number of boys and girls admitted to St Francis and Ramakrishna Mission Schools. I am working on many projects to promote education in this area. You must remember the feeling of my heart, which I have put into your bags with the reading and writing materials. Try not to forget it. You should always bear in mind that Swamiji wishes you to pursue your studies in the right spirit, earn something, serve society and then enter into family life. Entering into holy wedlock and producing children should be relegated to the last option. Marriage and children should never be your first priority. Try to remember that marriage and progeny should be your last priority. First is education, second is profession and third is production – marriage and progeny.

The problem is that these children have ambitions, but their parents are ill-bred and ill-informed. They can't see beyond their noses. The village girls of this area tend domestic cattle, collect the cow dung in the early morning, graze the cattle and goats and by the time they are eighteen or nineteen they are the mothers of two or three children. To beget a number of children was the necessity of the past, when our society was primitive and agriculture was the mainstay. Now the times have changed and children have ambitions. They talk among themselves of their dreams and ambitions. But their parents cannot see beyond begetting children. They don't know how to plan their families or how to make sacrifices for the well-being of their offspring.

There are many fathers who drink beyond their means and leave nothing for their wives and children. They say, "What will the children do after they have received higher education?" I asked one of the fathers to send his daughter to school. Quickly came the reply, "What will she do after getting an education? Will she do anything other than dealing with the cow dung?" This concept of education is very prevalent in society; it is not an insignificant concept.

To give is to share
This year I have involved the children in giving away prasad to the people gathered here as a means of training. Children should learn how to give, how to share their food with others.

Training in receiving is not essential because a child learns this in the mother's womb. So I don't give that training as children are born with it; they are trained graduates in that matter, past masters so to say. If children are trained in giving or sharing, they will learn how to give when they are grown up. I could have had the prasad distributed by any group of people, but I have involved the children in this work for their training. To give or share is an art. Give. To give is to share.

Satsang 12

December 17, 2001, Afternoon

*E*veryone has their *ishta devata*, their personal god. My ishta devata is Trayambakeshwar Mahadeva. Only twice in the past have I asked his permission, first in 1963 before going to Munger and again before coming to Rikhia. I went to Trayambakeshwar in December 1963 and prayed, "I am not having any breakthrough though I have studied the *Gita*, the Upanishads and other scriptures, and have served my guru with devotion. I am a learned man. I can discourse in Hindi, English and French and can speak with ease on any subject. I can talk on scientific topics, on moksha, on the Kamashastras and so on." I had this inflated ego but I was not getting any breakthrough.

I prayed to him and asked him to extend his helping hand for another twenty years and then see the results. "I will come to you after twenty years with some significant achievements" was the prayer and the vow I offered him in 1963. I had told him clearly that after twenty years I would come to him, leaving everything behind, and I did that in 1983. Whatever I had to do I had done by 1983. I had sowed the seed of yoga all over the world, I had prepared the seedlings and planted trees too. I had prepared a host of sannyasins to shoulder the responsibility. People all over the world had accepted the message of yoga.

117

In 1989, my task being fulfilled I visited Trayambakesh-war. I settled down in one of the rooms of the *goshala,* a cowshed, situated at the base of a hill named Neel Parvat. The room was small, five by ten, and I spent two months of the rainy season there very comfortably. Then I asked my ishta devata to tell me what to do. I had taken voluntary retirement with only a small bag as my total possession. I had no idea of the future and so I asked my ishta devata to show me the way.

During my stay in the goshala I drank milk twice a day, which someone used to bring for me. Some rotis were also sent but they did not attract me, so I had to manage with just the milk. Sometimes I would cook khichari in the evening on a stove in my small room. The room was dirty and dingy. I cleaned it thoroughly, removed two empty brandy bottles and made it liveable. I have the old habit of cleaning the premises and so I did that and stayed there for two months.

Receiving direction

On the fourth of September a great hurricane lashed the place. It passed through Maharashtra and caused large scale devastation in the coastal area of Gujarat. The same fateful night the message came as to what my future course of action would be, but I did not know where to begin. I had left Munger and had no intention of returning there. On the eighth of September I received an indication of the property opposite this one. I had a glimpse of the erect shirish and palash trees here and the word 'chitabhoomi' flashed. I had no difficulty then in identifying this area, because Deoghar is the cremation ground, the *chitabhoomi,* of Sati Parvati and Varanasi is the burial ground of Lord Shiva.

I decided to go to Deoghar and arrived here on the twenty-third of September 1989. Day and night are equal on that day. I had asked Swami Satsangi to go to Deoghar and purchase the property after locating the plot with these trees. I had described the physical features and asked her to find it. I had given her a broad idea of the chitabhoomi, which is a very large area. Who will find the shirish and palash trees in

118

an area the size of Deoghar district? She arrived in Deoghar and stayed in a hotel where she resolved to consult a knowledgeable priest the next day and try to find the spot with his help. Luckily next morning Giridhari Panda came across her. He is the priest of the nearby Harlajori temple. He took her to Rikhia and had the land registered the same day. Within three days she was given possession of the plot and she informed me by telephone. When I received this information I came here on the twenty-third of September 1989.

Forgotten promise

In 1983 I had met with a serious car accident in Australia, which very few people know about. I was immobilized and remained hospitalized for one and a half months. My gallbladder was punctured and one of my ribs was dislocated. I was not able to move from my hospital bed. It was a severe accident, but I did not tell anyone except Swami Niranjan. In India nobody knew about the accident. Even in Australia only two or three of the Australian swamis knew about this incident and I instructed them not to pass on the information to any one else.

Swami Niranjan asked permission to come and see me. I told him not to come because it was Australia and I was in no danger. The accident had occurred in the middle of a highway. I was rushed to the hospital immediately and all the necessary examinations were completed the same night. Next morning I moved to a nursing home. Had this accident taken place in any part of India, the result could have been fatal. Australian hospitals are fully equipped and everything was done within fifteen minutes in the emergency ward.

Later I returned to India via the Philippines. I had severe pain in my arms, legs and waist and could not undertake any physical exercise. From the Philippines I went to Mumbai and stayed at the Sun-n-Sand Hotel, where a friend had booked a room for me. It was in the Sun-n-Sand that the old vow flashed into my mind and I at once decided to go to Nasik to have darshan of my ishta devata. I took a taxi and went straight to Trayambakeshwar, accompanied by Swami Satsangi.

119

As soon as I bowed before the deity, the promise I had made and forgotten flashed into my memory. In December 1963 I had taken a vow to hasten to the service of my ishta devata as soon as my mission was fulfilled. But I had forgotten the vow. I had the ashram of my dream. I had achieved many things. The system of yoga I had developed had gained universal acceptance and recognition. The period of twenty years had elapsed and I was violating the promise I had taken in the presence of my ishta devata. During those twenty years I had worked like a bulldozer, moved through many countries, worked day and night and brought innumerable people into my fold. A lot of money came to me and I constructed many ashrams, but had forgotten the solemn vow I had taken in 1963. For this violation I had been punished in the form of that accident. As my memory revived I became aware of my guilt.

I was so deeply absorbed in thought that I forgot my incapacity and stepped straight into my car. My ailment had disappeared; I was one hundred percent cured. As soon as I had bowed my head to my ishta devata I had been reminded of the solemn vow. I finally decided to bid farewell to Munger. Then and there I realized the lapse on my part and the resulting penalty. I was fully recovered because I had realized my gross mistake. As soon as man realizes his mistake, divine grace comes.

God's grace

When you are in front of God you realize your own omissions and lapses very soon. When we really feel that we have made certain mistakes, God's grace comes. If man is guilty it is before God only; he is not responsible before any other authority. We are not at all guilty before any other person. I do not need to plead guilty before the police or the government. I have to confess my guilt before God alone. Thus I realized my gross mistake for I had not fulfilled the promise I had made to God. It had gone out of my mind. Why did I forget? Maya held me in her sway because success is also an illusion. When you achieve something, when you slide over the crest of success, you are possessed by maya. Success gives birth to intoxication and you forget the commitment, if any, you have made.

It is true that many yogashrams were established and the yogic movement had taken the world by storm. Knowledge of ancient India touched the shores of the oceans and many heads of religious institutions gave recognition to my school of thought and action. Medical scientists, scholars and psychologists, different opinion leaders and people at large recognized the theory and the method of my system of yoga. Besides this the Christian world at large and the Muslims of Iran and Iraq recognized the secular character of the yoga I preached and practised. All this went to my head and the illusory power of God, maya, took possession of me. I continued to postpone my departure from Munger. Tomorrow turned into today and the prophetic tomorrow never came.

When I was reminded of the commitment with a jolt, I hurried back to Munger and told Swami Niranjan of my resolve to finally quit Munger. I called my fast friend, the late Kedarnath Goenka, and disclosed to him my resolve to bid goodbye to Munger. He asked me my next destination. I told him that I would first go to Varanasi and from there to other places of pilgrimage to cleanse my head. My head was full of garbage, which I intended to remove. I bathed in the Ganga at Varanasi and went to Vindhyachal to have the holy glimpse of Mother Vindhyavasini. I had darshan of the deity three times and then I went to Pashupatinath in Kathmandu. I had the darshan of Lord Pashupatinath three times and then proceeded to Trayambakeshwar near Nasik. I have already told you about my experiences there.

In Trayambakeshwar

My stay at Trayambakeshwar for two months in 1989 was a very memorable one. I used to sit under a tree during the day. It was the time of the Kumbha Mela and a large number of sadhus and mendicants started gathering there to have a puff. It is a common sight in India. When sadhus gather at a

121

place they take a puff together. It has become customary, you can't prevent it. A puff is followed by tea, which was a difficult proposition for me. I requested the Acharya of the Math to discourage this habit as I was not there to take a puff and have cups of tea with those sadhus. He forbade them all from entering my room, otherwise they would come to smoke bidis and ganja and create a disturbance. I had to make tea many times for all those who visited my room. I was there to sing bhajans and do sadhana in isolation, but I couldn't follow my routine because of their frequent visits.

One companion

On coming to Rikhia I received the divine command that for sannyasins penance is a form of atonement for past deeds. A sannyasin has to make amends for all his accumulated deeds. So I undertook *panchagni,* the sadhana of the five fires, a very rigorous penance. My pet dog Bholenath was with me during my penance. Yesterday evening I kindled a lamp in his memory and chanted from the Koran at his samadhi – *Bismillah ir Rehman ir Rahim.* It was the anniversary of his death, and so I did all the rituals on that day. I loved him very much. I have never loved anyone in my life. I do not remember having loved even my parents or friends. I remember them only when a letter arrives. Otherwise I don't remember anyone. But I definitely remember him. This was one man – I am using the word 'man' for the dog – this was one creature who was with me all the twenty-four hours a day. Not even for a second did he stay away from me.

I have never spent twenty-four hours with any human being. I am a loner. Even now I live alone. Nobody shares my room, nobody peeps into my house. Someone comes in now and then to wash and clean it, but I do not have anybody with me. Only one creature ever lived with me twenty-four hours a day. He would get up with me, sit with me and also accompany me to the bathroom. When I sat to eat he would watch the movement of my mouth. When I watched his mouth for some time he was unable to understand what I was doing. Sometimes he would come closer to me and lick my mouth. He would gesture as if to ask, "What do you want?"

I have had no experience of companionship in my life except for this one, and that too was the companionship of a dog. Had I chosen any man, any boy or girl to be my companion, he or she would not have spent the entire day with me. Even if I turned over while lying on my bed, Bholenath knew. He was aware of me twenty-four hours a day. He did not leave me alone for even a second. In my whole life if I have spent twenty-four hours with any one, it is Bholenath. At night he used to sleep beside me. I never chained him up. He was a very ferocious dog. His presence is felt even today in Ganesha Kutir and nobody dares to step into it for fear of his ghost. No one enters my room without asking my permission. The ghost of Bholenath still reigns there.

Panchagni

Bholenath used to sit in the panchagni with me. The panchagni period is from the fourteenth of January to the sixth of July, from the winter equinox to the summer equinox. I had prepared mahabhasma to use during panchagni as prescribed in the *Devi Bhagavat Purana*. I covered my body with this specially prepared ash and I also used to bedaub his body with it. Bholenath was a pedigree Alsatian dog, a breed which is kept in an air-conditioned room during summer, but he was living with me within the heat range of panchagni. During panchagni the normal temperature was fifty degrees centigrade. Sometimes it rose to sixty degrees when a hot wind was blowing. Panchagni is a very difficult penance for which I had no experience. I am scared of heat, I can't tolerate it and I had my room air-conditioned in Munger. I am uncomfortable if the temperature goes beyond twenty or twenty-one degrees. So I lost hope of surviving when the mercury touched ninety degrees. But somehow I survived.

Kumbha Mela

Trayambakeshwar is located near the river Godavari. The Godavari originates from the hilltop at Trayambakeshwar.

The next Kumbha will be held in 2003 at Nasik. I went to the Kumbha Mela at Allahabad earlier this year at the time of Makar Sankranti, on the fourteenth of January. I arrived at night, took a bath in the early morning and left soon after. I caught the day train which reaches Allahabad at midnight. From the railway station I went straight to Triveni Sangam, took a bath and returned. From Deoghar to Trayamba-keshwar is a very long route. The direct train is from Calcutta.

Durga Saptashati

Now we shall listen to chanting from *Durga Saptashati*. Not only is chanting beneficial, but listening is equally beneficial. Try to read *Durga Saptashati*. In big cities people take French lessons and German lessons and in the same way you can also take *Durga Saptashati* lessons. Encourage your children to learn how to chant the *Durga Saptashati* mantras too. You may engage a tutor for this purpose and he will also learn something. It is so easy to chant. Try to learn it and start chanting in your home next year during Navaratri. The rules are not cumbersome. I do it every year. *Devi Suktam* is very easy to learn.

> *Ya devi sarvabhooteshu buddhiroopena samsthita*
> *Namastasyai namastasyai namastasyai namo namaha.*
> *Ya devi sarvabhooteshu nidraroopena samsthita*
> *Namastasyai namastasyai namastasyai namo namaha.*

You will only need to change one word in between like *kshuddha roopena, chhaya roopena, shakti roopena, lajja roopena* and so on. The other words remain as such. It won't take you very long to learn. Go on tilling the soil.

Finding a balance

In one year you may miss Simla and Ooty and spend that time observing Navaratri. You should try to strike a balance between the two extremes. You may go on pleasure trips during other vacations and do the chanting during Navaratri. This will bring about balance in your life. If you go on eating and eating without fasting your bowels will be upset. To

124

strike a balance you should fast. In the same way the rubbish accumulated in your system will be cleansed if you observe Navaratri every year. After this cleansing operation you may go to Ooty or another hill station and get a refill of garbage in your system. So balance is very essential in life.

There are four aims of human existence: *artha, kama, dharma* and *moksha* – worldly riches, sensual enjoyment religious merit and liberation, or the state of perfect and perpetual calm. Of those four aims two are of one nature and the other two are of a different nature. If you fail to understand this truth you will remain in a state of sorrow for your whole life. In truth also there is balance. Wherever you go you will see balance. Even in cycling you require balance or else you will fall. Unless you strike a balance in your life, you will not be able to achieve anything.

You have come here to achieve that balance. You have suffered a life of pain and pleasure for three hundred and sixty days of the year. The remaining five days of the year which you spend here will be free from pain and pleasure. Where there is neither pleasure nor pain there is bliss, ananda. Therefore, my name is ananda – I am free from pain and pleasure. I am in perpetual and perfect bliss. Every swami's name ends in ananda – Swami Satyananda, Swami Niranjanananda and so on. Ananda or bliss is a state where pain and pleasure are equibalanced. You have the same feeling both in pleasure and in pain. You remain here in perfect bliss.

A visit to Rikhia is not a pleasure. You are blessed to be here. How will you describe this bliss? How will a deaf and dumb person describe the experience of tasting sugar candy? This is bliss. The sound and vibration created by the chanting rescmbles the humming of the black bee. The black bees sing in this manner. The acharyas are chanting mantras from the *Rig Veda* and *Yajur Veda*, *Atharva Veda* and *Sama Veda*. These sounds were produced by our sages and seers thousands of years ago when people in other parts of the globe used to walk naked. While the people residing in other parts of the world were eating fowl and partridge our sages and seers were

125

chanting the mantras of the Vedas. They designed the rules of versification and metre and made the Vedic mantras fit to be sung. It is so sweet and melodious to hear.

Now let the worship begin. Humility is the way to self-defence. The world could be conquered by humility. Gandhi won freedom for India by means of the spinning wheel. But today in Kosovo and Afghanistan even gunfire is not working. Please remember this. Sometimes you are constrained to use firearms in self-defence. Dark forces can be vanquished only by using matching forces.

Yoga – a world culture

We have resolved to perform the Rajasooya Yajna for twelve years. We can perform Vishnu Yajna or Rudra Yajna in the course of the Rajasooya Yajna, but we have made Sat Chandi Yajna our base. Only those persons are entitled to perform Rajasooya Yajna who have conquered the whole world, who have vanquished all the surrounding kings and emperors. I have not vanquished kings and emperors, but the yoga victory campaign which I started from Munger in 1964 had touched all the big towns and cities of the world by 1983. I unfurled the flag of yogic victory in all the important cities of the world in a period of twenty years. Today yoga has been recognized and included as a subject in the syllabus of universities, medical colleges, research centres, psychological institutions, jails and national and multinational companies. Nobody has challenged the theory and practice of yoga that I propounded. Now yoga is a universally accepted world culture.

My greatest achievement is the establishment of the first University of Yoga at Munger, which has been duly recognized by the University Grants Commission. Bihar Yoga Bharati is not an ordinary university. Students from east, west, north and south come for undergraduate courses and postgraduate degrees. Armed with the degrees of this university they will obtain employment in institutions and organizations in their countries. Wouldn't you call it a victory over the world? This is not the age of the sword, this is the age of intellect. This is the age of the expansion of mental horizons.

It is for this reason that I am sowing the seed of the Rajasooya Yajna. Now Swami Satyananda declares himself a victor of the world. I kept quiet for many years. I came to Deoghar to cast off this mortal coil. I underwent a fiery ordeal. Can anybody survive after practising panchagni, the austerity of sitting in the sun surrounded on all sides by burning fire? It is not at all possible to survive in the heat generated by five sacred fires, which varied between sixty, seventy, eighty and ninety degrees centigrade. Sitting in that scorching fire from the fourteenth of January to the sixteenth of July is no joke, but I did not succumb to the fatal heat; I was not dehydrated even for a day. I said to myself, "Swami Satyananda, you have one thing in your mind, but God has something else in His mind." Then I decided to perform yajnas. I did yajnas in the first year, second year and third year without any show. It was all a simple affair.

This year is the first year of the Rajasooya Yajna. It will be repeated in subsequent years and conclude in the twelfth year. In Rajasooya Yajna three things are very important – worship, satsang and offering gifts. You offer to Devi and I offer it back as Devi's prasad. The sweets you present to the deity in a temple are given back to you as prasad. You present your offerings to the Divine Mother and the Divine Mother gives you Her prasad in return. The prasad I have distributed today were the offerings made by you to the Divine Mother. You have made all the offerings.

Satsang 13

December 18, 2001, Morning

A yajna has three important parts. The first is satsang, where you sing kirtan, hear spiritual pronouncements and spiritual ideas. We have had Devi kirtan followed by the recitation from *Ramayana*, then guru pooja, which is considered to be the most important aspect of spiritual life. Worship of guru precedes everything. After that comes the second part of yajna, which is the main ritual, the worship of Devi, with mantra, yantra and mandala. That is the tantric system of worship.

The third important part of yajna as enunciated by our ancestors is to give. I am using the word give not charity. In Sanskrit it is known as daan. Charity and daan are not synonymous. Daan presupposes that giving and taking are balanced. Balanced give and take is daan. This is a very important part of the yajna. A yajna without daan is incomplete. That daan is a token prasad from Devi; it is not charity given to a poor man because nobody is poor. It is the prasad of Devi which is given to all of us. The meaning of this offering is taken very lightly these days. People learn to take in their mother's womb, but they learn to offer from their gurus, their teachers. Yajnas teach us about offering.

What does prasad mean? Prasad means pleasure, happiness. It is the reverse of pain and sorrow. So it is

128

happiness. Prasad does not mean presents or gifts – prasad means happiness. That which causes elation in your heart, which makes you very happy, is called prasad. Devi gives you happiness in the form of a lehnga and choli, in the form of a dhoti and a sari. I have been given these things and I am so happy! I am so happy because it was Her prasad that I was given. So these are the three parts of yajna.

Kingdom of yoga

We have been holding Sat Chandi Yajna since 1995, but this is the first year of the Rajasooya Yajna. Only one who has conquered the four corners of the world can perform this yajna. Swami Satyananda is really a digvijayi. He has conquered the seven seas, not politically, but by virtue of his yogadanda he has been successful in spreading and establishing the power of yoga throughout the world. I never understood politics. I am not a person with rajadanda, the power of ruling; rather I am a man with yogadanda, the power of yoga. My guru told me to spread and teach yoga throughout the world and I did that. No one dared to challenge me in this field, neither religious leaders, sceptics or agnostics. I didn't face any challenge in Russia or China, in America or from the Vatican. I did not face any challenge anywhere in the world. There was no country where I did not train someone in yoga. People bowed before me, offered me their sons and daughters to help spread yoga and donated generously to this cause. I have received the love, affection and cooperation of people everywhere.

The first university of yoga in the world has been started in Munger. It has been recognized by the University Grants Commission and the Ministry of Human Resource Development of the Government of India. This unique university teaches yoga up to postgraduate level. All the university teachers are well qualified; some are retired and have taught in universities elsewhere. They are not only from the four corners of this country but from other parts of the world too. These qualified teachers teach Yoga Philosophy, Yoga Psychology, Applied Yoga Science and various other subjects.

129

People come here from all over the world, including Korea, Argentina and Iran. You can see them sitting here. There are no political differences here. As far as yoga is concerned we are one nation and this is the message that we have been able to spread throughout the world.

The importance of clothing

The distribution of prasad will begin now. We do not call it daan, donation, we call it prasad, offering. Why is clothing being offered as prasad? As I explained to you the other day I learnt the significance of cloth from Gandhi. I had been a witness to the Independence Movement of Mahatma Gandhi from early childhood. Gandhi exhorted people to take recourse to the spinning wheel, the *charkha*, to make India an independent nation. People often questioned his wisdom. They talked about achieving freedom through the bullet of a gun and here the Mahatma was exhorting people to take up the spinning wheel in order to gain freedom from foreign rule. Nobody thought freedom could be achieved without the power of the gun. Only one man thought of achieving freedom through non-violent means and that man was Mahatma Gandhi. Now think about why he did that? Thread comes out of a spinning wheel and cloth is made from it. You can remain without food and water for a day or two, but everyone needs clothing twenty-four hours a day. This was the mantra, the key point, of Mahatma Gandhi.

I had been thinking about what Devi's prasad should be. Should it be gold or silver or sweetmeats? No, that wouldn't be proper. I asked everybody here; they all had different views. So I asked Bapuji. Gandhi used to arrange for clothes. So I decided to offer saris, lehnga-cholis, towels, underwear and the like as Devi's prasad, according to Gandhi's formula. I have requisitioned clothes from all over India. These have come all the way from Kutch, Meghalaya, Assam, Nagaland, Bengal, North India, South India – from all the four corners of this country and are being offered as prasad to everyone present here. One can get these things from the market too, but this idea is quite different. You have to think about the

130

relationship of clothing to a human being and to employment. You have to understand the importance of clothing, which we all wear twenty-four hours a day. Since every one of us needs clothes, their consumption too must be very great. So the textile industry, the clothing industry, is a very important industry. That is the concept of Mahatma Gandhi.

Feeling oneness
That is the basis of this prasad. You will all be leaving here in a day or two. Then my job will be to deliver tractor loads of this prasad to the adjoining villages who need these blankets, clothes, lanterns, kerosene oil, umbrellas, raincoats and so on, so much. It is written in Vedanta, in our Upanishads, that all of us, living or dead, are part of the universal soul which resides within all of us. It is very easy to say that, but in actual practice we do not follow that tenet. In practice 'I' is separate from 'you'. The feeling of oneness comes when you can feel that all those who live around you have the same soul or are part of the same soul that is within you and that their sorrow and pleasure are your own sorrow and pleasure.

It may not be possible for me as a human being to share all the difficulties of my neighbours, but certainly I should have the quality to feel that. One person like me cannot wipe out the pain of everyone in the world. I am not God. As a man, I have my limitations. But there should be the feeling that if your child is sick, I should feel the pain that you feel for your child, or for that matter the pain of your friends, wife, daughters and neighbours, in the same way as I would for my own kith and kin. This is very important. The sayings of the Upanishads will not be true until one practises that. It is no use saying that everyone is myself. You should feel that everyone is yourself, then you will feel their problems.

Relationship with the local people
I have completed twelve years of my stay here and during this period the conditions of the people in this panchayat have improved remarkably. You might all have witnessed

that change. There is almost one hundred percent education among the children. Every one of them now goes to school. I have told the widows to wear clothes similar to normal married women and have offered them such clothes to wear. Girls have been provided with bicycles so they can go to Deoghar for schooling safely. The level of education is very high here and the chosen language of this area is English. These girls come from the families of labourers, rickshaw pullers, coolies, ploughmen, transplanters, weavers and tailors; they are not the children of office workers.

We utilize the services of the villagers for brickmaking, carpentry, housing construction, welding – everything is done here locally. We do not hire people from Deoghar or any other town now. If our water pump is out of order, then the mechanic comes from a nearby village to repair it. The painting, whitewashing, electrical works, every item of work is taken care of by local artisans. We have established a relationship with these rural people. I often go for a stroll to these villages, sometimes one way and sometimes the other way. People watch out for me and the children say good morning to me. If somehow they miss seeing me, then the children start shouting at their parents, "Mummy, Papa, Swamiji has gone past." It is not because I give them anything. As a matter of fact, love is quite reciprocal. When you love someone you receive the same amount of love in return. If I ignore you, then you are bound to ignore me too.

Munger representatives
About three to four hundred people from Munger have come here to work during this yajna. The children in red shirts are all from Munger town. Some are staying in dharmashalas and in the villages with the local people. Every morning they report for duty to clean and prepare the premises for the day's proceedings. I lived in Munger for twenty years, from 1963 to 1983, and I used to teach the people yoga techniques. They have imbibed the yogic way of life. The Munger Yoga Mitra Mandal is very big. The delegation from Munger is the largest one here. These people

do not have an ashram in Munger town. Bal Yoga Mitra Mandal (Children's Yoga Fellowship), Yuva Yoga Mitra Mandal (Youth Yoga Fellowship) and their associate members come from the areas around the town and number three to four thousand. This is a very strong force. Every one of them has come here to work as their participation is quite important for this yajna.

Marriage

Every year we choose an eligible bride and bridegroom for this occasion. In previous years they have been chosen from Greece, Ireland, Spain and India. The Rama and Sita of this year are from India. This year's Rama is the son of Krishna Devi Mishra, the *manaskokila*, who gives discourses from the *Ramayana* and sings the praises of Lord Rama. She is a renowned 'Ramayani'. Stand up so that people can see you. Sitaji should stand up too. Show your face. In India when the daughter-in-law shows her face for the first time it is called 'showing the face', otherwise she is veiled. When she shows her face you have to offer her something. So they offer gold, silver and pearl, not platinum. All the women of the community come and look. They say, "Oh, she is like Lakshmi," "Oh, she is like Saraswati," but nobody says she is like Kali! They give all kinds of compliments.

As a child the bridegroom used to dance a lot. Now he is quite grown up and works as a sales executive in a big company. Do they pay you well? Can you maintain her without seeking financial assistance from your mother and father? He is becoming serious now because once you are caught in marriage, you become very serious. You become very careful because you don't know what kind of lady she is going to be! Before marriage the bridegroom is often very talkative, never behaving very seriously, but suddenly after his marriage, he mends his ways and becomes dignified. Now, it is not certain whether that happens by itself or if the wife plays a role. You people know better than I do. I have little experience of it as there was no one to make me dignified.

133

I am not against marriage. My position is that before marriage a girl should be allowed to pursue her studies, then choose her own profession. Once she starts earning her living, she will have self-respect and be self-supporting. After that, she may marry at the age of twenty-five to thirty years, if she needs to at all. If she does not feel like marrying, then we are there to take care of such women as sannyasins.

Sannyasa and family life

There are two ashrams – sannyasa and grihastha, family life. An ashram is a place where one labours to fulfil a mission. In our vocabulary it denotes a place of endeavour and there are several types of endeavour. Learning, renunciation, maintaining and being part of a family, business, rearing children, bearing pain and enjoying pleasure are all the domains of such endeavour. When someone makes an effort to remove the pain of others without taking care of their own difficulties first, such an endeavour is called renunciation. This often happens in a family when the mother does everything possible to remove the pain of her children without thinking of her own difficulties. This is one aspect of her sacrifice. In the homes of the deprived, one often sees the mother offering all the food to her children and taking little or nothing for herself. This, too, is a great thing.

Hence, whether it is family life or sannyasa life, the values are the same except that the ways and positioning may be slightly different. This change is due to the time, place and space. Swami Niranjan and Swami Satsangi have renounced for the well-being of mankind. On a smaller scale, a householder also sacrifices his own freedom for the cause of the dependants in the family. Tolerance, compassion, forgiveness, honouring another's viewpoint – these values are usually common wherever you live in a society.

I do not want to differentiate between householders and sannyasins. That is why I have always said that sannyasa and family life should not be viewed separately. We do not see them as being antagonistic to each other and they are never diametrically opposed to each other. We have in our fold

134

several sannyasins with families and children. This does not mean that I ask sannyasins to get married. The dictum of the shastras is clear and hence as far as is practicable, one should remain a celibate.

There is an old saying. A sannyasin is *Alakh Niranjan*, a pious soul. If there are two, things become complicated – *latpat*; if there are three, things go topsy-turvy – *gadbad*; and if there are four, rest assured the game will be spoiled – *choupat!* As far as practicable sannyasins should live alone and follow brahmacharya. This is always essential. A sannyasin must avoid proximity to other men or women. This saying from the shastras should be followed. But sometimes if one of the sannyasins goes off to lead a householder's life, I do not treat him as fallen or as an outcast; rather I say that instead of a swami he has now become a *goswami*, which is a title given to pandits and priests. Even if a sannyasin marries he should not quit his sannyasa dharma.

Atri and Anusooya

Such people who become householders are treated in the category of rishis. We have several such rishis and the names of Sati Anusooya and her husband Atri often come to mind. Their son was Dattatreya, one of the greatest avadhootas, who represented the trinity – Brahma, Vishnu and Mahadeva. It is said that he was the incarnation of Brahma, Hari and Shiva. Such was the greatness of Dattatreya Avadhoota! Atri and Anusooya were the parents of Dattatreya. Atri was a rishi, Anusooya was his wife. Rishi Atri was debauched. He had a wife but he used to go to a prostitute. I hope you all know the story. When Atri became incapacitated and couldn't walk, Anusooya would carry him on her shoulders to the prostitute every evening. He would spend the night there and in the morning Anusooya would carry him home. The son born to them was Dattatreya, the great yogi, the founder of a sannyasa sect, the great siddha. All sannyasins in India pay absolute homage to that man, who was the son of a debauched father.

There are several stories about them which can be found in the *Mahabharata* or Puranas. Once Anusooya commanded the sun not to rise and the sun did not rise. This Anusooya gave birth to such a great son to whom she preached renunciation. Sati Anusooya preached to Lord Rama when he was moving from Chitrakoot to Dandakaranya. She preached to Sita too and also offered her clothes. These were the clothes that Sita wore in captivity in her Lanka abode. Such was the quality of the clothes that Sita was able to use them for so long without washing them.

Search for goodness

I am talking about householders and sannyasins and I do not find any difference between the two. Householders must give respect to sannyasins and vice versa. Sannyasins should not think that householders are fallen people and similarly householders should not think of sannyasins as cheats. It is true, however, that some people say that people in yellow or in the garb of sannyasins are cheats. This is very bad. Such things are politically motivated, where one side wants to show the other as being very bad. You will often hear people talking about officials as being corrupt, businessmen as being crooked, labourers as being cheats and even sannyasins as being imposters. Who then is good? These days people say that traders are thieves, the leaders are corrupt, the ministers are crooked. You are talking about a society in which no one is supposed to be good. No society can survive in this way. You will have to look for good people in every society. You will have to search for goodness. There are many good saints in the world. Only a few people are bad; bad people are not large in number.

You must think about this point – this world is based on righteousness, on dharma. It is being run on the basis of honesty. This world moves on faith. You should understand this fully. If this world were devoid of good people, it would become a jungle. There is no dearth of good people here. The preponderance of good to bad is like a kilogram of vegetables with a quinine tablet in it. No sooner do you taste

136

the vegetables than you feel something is bitter and declare that all the vegetables are bad. This world is not like that. If you find a hair in your food, it does not mean that all the food is full of hairs. Take out that strand of hair and the food will be as good as ever. In the same way, this world has a lot of truth, dharma, righteousness, faith and trust. That is why this world survives. We are not thieves and you are not thieves.

Chanting

I have received a lot of copies of the books *Devi Mahatmya* and *Japa Yoga* from my guru's ashram in Rishikesh. *Devi Mahatmya* will be distributed to people from overseas. It was written by my guru, Swami Sivananda, who used to write in English. The other book, *Japa Yoga*, has been translated and every villager has been offered a copy so that they too can do some meditation practices. When you come to chant *Ramacharitamanas* tomorrow, the book will be yours to keep. You need not return it. In the same manner, you may take *Durga Saptashati* with you, which will help you to perform Navaratri in your homes every year.

You should make a resolve to chant at least one *doha*, one couplet, daily from *Ramacharitamanas*. It will bring happiness and prosperity to your domestic life. You will receive the blessings of the saints and sages through chanting *Ramacharitamanas*. To start with recite the Mangalacharan, the opening sloka of Balakanda, then the first *soratha*: *"Jehi sumirat sidhi hoi, gananaayaka karibara badana."* Thereafter, *"Bhaya pragata kripaalaa deenadayaalaa, kaushalyaa hitakaari"* and then recite a doha and finally the arati. If you can't invest even fifteen minutes in your own happiness, peace and prosperity then who will help you? Even God can't come to your rescue.

Four Ganeshas

I live in Ganesha Kutir where I have placed four different Ganeshas. One is Ganesha Ramani, who represents the working class. He is the representative of the scheduled

137

castes and tribes, so I have given him the name Ganesha Ramani. Then there is Ganesha Iyer, who is in my room because my guru was an Iyer. His name was Dr Kuppuswami Iyer before he took sannyasa. So I have given the name Ganesha Iyer to the statue in my bedroom. The third one is named Ganesha Bhattacharya, because Bengalis are good at cooking and eating and hence I have given this Bengali brahmin name to this statue.

I don't cook very much now, but for six years I used to cook my own food. Even today when the food in the kitchen is not to my taste, I cook something for myself. The new cooks who came recently were using a lot of condiments and so I refused to eat that food. At my age, and for that matter at any age, a person should not eat condiments very much – and at this age if one were to take them would he remain alive? One has to discriminate between the taste and the effect!

The fourth statue of Ganesha is kept in a secluded area and has the name Ganesha Ali. I am not joking. I take this seriously. Why can't Ganesha become a Muslim? Ganesha has several faces. We have only four here and we worship and pray before them. We offer them incense and candles every morning and evening.

When Chaturmas begins, after Karka Sankranti, anushthana is performed for four months. Whatever anushthana we begin will be completed during the period of the bright moon in the month of Kartik on *Devauthani Ekadashi,* the awakening of the devatas. It is the eleventh day of the lunar calendar. On that day I perform pooja and finish the prescribed anushthana. Then we worship and offer prasad to Ganesha. Whatever prasad we offer to him on this auspicious day is then given to others.

Prasad from Ganesha and Devi
Since 1990, whatever is offered to Ganesha is distributed to everyone here, be it a cycle, a rickshaw, a sewing machine or clothes. The process of offering is very simple. Before we offer these things to the Goddess, we prepare a list. We then

138

pray that after the articles have been offered to Her, they will be distributed as prasad from Her to the people who need them the most. Once She okays it, they are distributed. This year, as the materials to be offered were so many that I had neither the time nor the space to move inside Ganesha Kutir, I asked Ganesha to take care of these articles. When the invocation began on the fifteenth, all the materials were brought here and with the beginning of the first chapter of *Durga Saptashati*, everything was offered to the Mother Goddess. Now this prasad has two seals – one from Ganesha and the other from Devi.

In Kali Yuga, we recognize only two main authorities. One is Ganesha and the second is Mother Chandi. These are the deities of Kali Yuga. In each age the deities are different. In Satya Yuga there was Indra, Varuna and the like. The prasad you are receiving is from the deities of this age, Chandi and Vinayaka, and it has the seal of these two authorities. This is the tradition of prasad. Every year we have such a tradition. Fifty percent of the rickshaws and thelas that you see in and around Deoghar have been donated by this akhara to needy people. The people who have been offered these earn fifty rupees every day.

Providing basic needs is a duty

As you know, money has three destinations: *daan*, offering; *bhoga*, enjoyment; and *nasha*, destruction. All property has these three destinations only. You may enjoy it or you may offer it, otherwise it will be lost or destroyed. Anything and everything, movable or immovable, gold or silver, food or sweetmeats, clothes or animals, cars or anything else. So you should think about how much you need for your own enjoyment. How can I wear so many clothes? What will I do with these gold and silver ornaments? To collect and keep things is not enjoyment; to store things is also not enjoyment. Enjoyment is utilizing things for oneself. You may require a life of comfort and for that you may need a refrigerator, an air conditioner, a good television set, a heater, a hot water geyser and so on. But besides these, you have many other

139

things that you do not need and such things you must offer to the needy. This should not be done as charity. If you offer a job or service to the needy, or if you make a firm arrangement for the livelihood of a needy person, you will be doing yeoman service to that family.

There was a driver with this ashram who stayed with us for two or three years. Then we arranged an auto rickshaw for him and now he is self-sufficient and earns his own living of one hundred rupees a day. If he fails to earn his living after we have made these arrangements we can do little, because it is due to fate. We are satisfied that we did what had to be done. If a labourer earns forty or fifty rupees a day, it is not very much. Now such people who earn this way are capable of making both ends meet. It is the duty of each one of us, be it the ruler or the ruled, to see that no one is deprived of this basic minimum need.

Sannyasins have this duty uppermost as this society has also reared sannyasins from time immemorial All those sannyasins who have shaved their heads or who are initiated must listen to this. A sannyasin cannot be a symbol of enjoyment – he can never be that. A sannyasin is not a consumer. He is a trustee. Sannyasins are always rich, sannyasins are never poor, but their riches do not belong to them. A sannyasin can only be a trustee. Whatever we get we keep in trust. That is the trust of this society and nobody has the right to breach the trust.

Emergence of poverty

In every age, the need of society has changed. In all the scriptures and books I have read, I have not come across any mention of the poverty of the people. There are thousands of books from the time of Buddha and poverty is never mentioned. But during the last one hundred to one hundred and fifty years, after the Industrial Revolution, when the common people were deprived of and forced to lose their arts and crafts, they became poor. In any newspaper, magazine or book you will find two common issues depicted – poverty and corruption. Everyone talks

140

about these two issues. Even jokes are rampant on these two topics. That means these problems are of a recent nature.

I have read *Akbar Nama, Babar Nama,* about Alamgir and also about the reign and times of Chandragupta Maurya, Ashoka and so on, and nowhere is poverty mentioned, although other problems of war and conflict are mentioned. References to poverty do not appear during the Ramayana period or during the period of the Puranas. It does not appear in the *Mahabharata* nor in *Banddha Charita.* You do not find it either during the Maurya or Mughal periods. Poverty has come after the British period because of the prevalence of big industries which destroyed the rural economy in which smaller artisans survived. The market economy is the mother of poverty. But we can do little about that. I am not criticizing it. I am just narrating the facts and nobody can change the facts. You can't change that large market economy. I can't change it, nobody can change it, because it is what the powerful people of this world want.

Responsibility of sannyasins to society

The brahmins, meaning the intellectuals, do not rule nations today, nor do the kshatriyas, meaning weapon holders. Today the world is ruled by the business and working classes. But each one of us should remember that the sannyasins do have a special responsibility in this age. Otherwise sannyasins would be at liberty to stay in the forests or in their ashrams and worship as they liked. Their disciples would come to them and satsang would go on. Sannyasins used to dwell in solitude – that was our culture. Kings and emperors used to bow before them and receive their counsel and blessings. But now that is no more.

Today sannyasins are the most powerful wing of society. A sannyasin can manage a panchayat alone, neither a Deputy Commissioner nor a Superintendent of Police is required. Rajadanda, the authority of the ruler, has failed to manage society. If it had been capable, then what you saw in Afghanistan, Kosovo or Croatia or Bosnia might not have happened. If the authority of the state had been capable,

141

such a situation would not have occurred there. This authority of the state is quite incapable of managing. But yogadanda, the power of yoga, can manage it. Yogadanda means that the sannyasins and the people live together in a community. In a panchayat there are about eight to ten thousand people. Of these, four to five thousand are men and women living together and the rest are children. You have to take care of their food and education. There is the possibility of all the children aged six to fifteen living with us in the ashram. Any sannyasin can do that. Even today in this country people have great faith and trust in the sannyasins.

Sannyasins are emperors without crowns. All the children over six years of age can stay in an ashram. They can have their meals there and study up to senior Cambridge level. Once they reach that level of education, some can return home and become householders and look after their hearth and home, their cattle and so on. Those with the aspiration can pursue further higher studies. Sannyasins will now have to dedicate themselves to the upliftment of society. If this is not done, then the deprived section of the community will destroy both the rulers and the sannyasins. They will not allow them to survive.

Changing needs of society

What is happening in Europe? The Christian religion is almost breathing its last. Why? European society does not require bread and butter; it does not need the hospitals that we need here. European society needs spiritual leaders like Swami Vivekananda, Bhaktivedanta, Maharishi Mahesh Yogi and the like. They are required there. You have to quickly identify the requirements of a society. What is needed in Europe, in England, we do not need in India. We need schools and colleges, hospitals and gurukuls, and they need yoga, meditation, the Upanishads, Bhagavat and gurus. You can see this with your own eyes.

Every society has separate needs. What America needs, India does not need and what is needed in India, America does not want. Sannyasins will have to acquire that

142

understanding. Swami Vivekananda understood that; he was a brilliant person. Maharishi Mahesh Yogi also understands that. Are you aware that he runs six channels from Holland, one of which is free? We have all these channels here. Swami Satsangi is a student of his Open University. She downloads all the required information on her computer during the day and goes through it in the evening. She passes all the prescribed examinations. She reads all about the Vedas, Puranas, the theory of Ayurveda and all the thoughts of ancient India which are almost lost to the world. She learns through these channels of Mahesh Yogi.

Our children are not aware of the cardinal ancient thoughts of India. The Indian people and their leaders, the teachers, professors, officers and those holding high positions, know nothing about it. But in England and America, through these gurus and sages who have gone there from India, people have started learning about the treasures of the shastras – Ayurveda, Atharva Veda, Vaidyaka, Rasayana, Jyotish and so many more. If I were to tell you about them you would all find it hard to believe that our ancestors possessed so much knowledge. You wouldn't believe it because you are in the realm of calculating two into two.

So I tell the sannyasins that our front has now changed. It is not only Swami Satyananda who provides practical commodities to the villagers. I am just a sannyasin and a sannyasin is a preceptor of knowledge. Sannyasins are meant to teach yoga, to show the way to samadhi, to pave the way for liberation. Our ancestors prescribed that for us, not for distributing rickshaws and thelas. Our ancestors did not formulate the path of sannyasa for these mundane works. The only path that sannyasins were meant to follow was showing people the spiritual way, guiding people towards spirituality. But the situation here and now is so grave that we, the sannyasins, will have to start right from scratch.

Understanding rural culture
Those who rule know nothing about the people. There are many villagers around us in whose homes there is nothing

to eat. I became aware of this when Swami Satsangi, in whose able hands this institution runs, told me about the pitiable conditions of the people around me. When she visited the homes of the people around this ashram only then could I understand their conditions and I thought, "My God, how do they live and survive?" She too could not fathom how they lived. One evening she returned from their homes and bemoaned, "Swamiji, I have learnt that there was no food for the night in the neighbouring home." I told her to do what she thought was best. She used to send rice, pulse, oil and condiments to such houses and people started arriving at her door.

Swami Satsangi is the actual founder of this institution in every way, monetarily and administratively. It is her dream. When Swami Satsangi left her job, she received a large gratuity. She also had a big apartment of her own in Bombay. When she sold everything the amount was quite large so she started constructing buildings here, of course, in the name of Bihar School of Yoga, not in her own name. In the first few years she worked very hard building and learning about rural life. Then Bihar School of Yoga and Sivananda Math came forward to assist her. She has become an asset for the people here and they like her.

When Swami Satsangi first came to Rikhia she was completely ignorant of rural India and rural life. She comes from that generation in India where girls today prefer to 'snack and dance', put on a Michael Jackson CD. She knew all about that culture. She had no idea about rural culture, but since she was living here with me, naturally she had to attune herself to these surroundings. Swami Satsangi was so ignorant of rural life that she did not know the difference between a cow and a bull! She did not know how the people in rural India lived. Now she knows everything, the ABCD of everything, totally.

At the same time, however, she has a very strong personality. She gives out to everyone right and left. There is no question of formality and talks. She calls a rose a rose and a spade a spade. A person who shoulders responsibility should be very strong. Of course, after me she will carry on the work of Sivananda Math very well. I don't deal with the management, planning or administration of this place at all. Initially I used to tell her what to do, but not now.

There are hundreds of thousands of people in our society who do not get the right food. The number of such deprived people is very large in India. You are at liberty to speak high sounding words, but the fact remains that there are many people in this country whose children are deprived of the food they need. What should our duty be towards them? A citizen and a sannyasin have to think about their duty towards such people. I was trained by my guru to preach, but what is my duty in this changed situation? We have to look at that. Then we also have to be aware that if we do not do our duty, the deprived section of society may not allow us to live in their society, as has happened in foreign countries where Christianity is breathing its last.

Satsang 14

December 18, 2001, Afternoon

$\mathcal{W}$ hat a saint Prabhupada Bhakti Vedanta was – fantastic! By chanting *'Hare Rama Hare Rama Rama Rama Hare Hare Hare Krishna Hare Krishna Krishna Krishna Hare Hare'* he revolutionized the power of devotion towards the Almighty throughout the West. Swami Vivekananda, Swami Ramatirtha, Swami Sivananda, Anandamayi Ma and Neem Karoli Baba – you will find their disciples everywhere. Wherever you go, their disciples will identify themselves by telling you that they are their followers. By reflecting on their great deeds, we take care of our neighbours during this yajna. Wherever we might be, we simply pray to God to let us be a medium for His mission. The will of God is implemented through a medium. With these thoughts in mind we are watching what He has in store for us. Now my age is also very great and I don't have any special wish to stay longer. I often have the feeling that if I departed early, I may have the opportunity to return sooner. If I were to depart now, then I may get an opportunity to return in five or ten years, and such a return would be quite refreshing!

Bholenath – the best disciple

Until two years ago I had a dog with me, the only disciple who comes to my mind and memory. Frankly speaking, I

146

don't remember anyone else. I remember Bholenath because I have never had a disciple like him. He represented what a disciple should be. He was aware of me all the time. One hour has sixty minutes, each minute has sixty seconds and he was aware of me every second. He did not miss a second. If I went to the bathroom he would come too. When I went to sleep at night every now and then he would come and sniff to see if I was there or not. He would not leave me alone, or rather he was not prepared to be left alone. Bholenath represented the best in a disciple. Every disciple, every devotee, must remember God all the time.

I also served him very well. I broke all the rules of an ashram. He was not a vegetarian; he ate nothing but meat. If you gave him rotis he would not touch them. He would not even look at rice, dal or vegetables. All he liked was milk, cheese, butter and meat, nothing else. I used to cook his meat for him. The Greek people gave me a cooking pot, which I would put on at two in the morning and by two in the afternoon the meat would be ready. I never cooked for myself, but I used to cook for him, and he knew it. Afterwards he would lick my feet, which meant, "Thank you, Swamiji."

It is a funny story because I am not a dog lover. I may be a God lover but not a dog lover. Swami Niranjan is a dog lover. One day in 1989 he came here from Munger with the pup, which was only a few months old, and showed him to me proudly. He said, "Swamiji, this is my dog," and I said, "Very nice." The dog was scratching all day because he had scabies. In Munger he was eating the same food as everybody else in the ashram. I said, "He is going to die if you don't feed him properly." Swami Niranjan said he couldn't feed him meat as in the Munger ashram people come from all sects and beliefs. So I said, "Leave him here, because Swami Satyananda does not care about anyone's criticism. I will do what I think is right, whether people like it or not. If people do not want to come here because I am cooking meat for the dog I will be the happiest person because that's what I want – to be all alone."

147

In Deoghar I got in touch with a Muslim butcher. I started with fifty grams of meat and the pup's scabies went away. He developed by day and by night. I gave him the name Bholenath. He became very strong, so I said, "Bhole-nath needs Bhairavi also." So we got a female dog from Orissa, the daughter of a police dog; her father or mother was an 'inspector'. These people from Orissa loved Bhairavi so much that they would bow down to her just like you bow down in a temple. She died only recently. She was the companion of Bholenath.

Intensity of devotion
Bholenath only took about two and a half minutes to eat his meal, with one eye on the meat and one eye on me. I had to stand there all the time because if I moved he would leave his food. This is how a devotee has to feel about God and this is how a disciple has to keep the guru in mind. How much do you love God? As much as my dog loved me? How much do you think about God? As much as my dog thought about me? How much are you aware of God? All the time? As much as my dog was aware of me, twenty-four hours a day, every minute and every second? There was not even one second when he was not aware of his master, Swami Satyananda.

In the *Ramacharitamanas* Tulsidas prays that Lord Rama should remain as dear to him as a woman is to a lustful person or as gold and money are to a greedy person.

*Kamihi nari piyari jimi lobhihi priya jimi daam
Timi Raghunath nirantara priya lagahu mohi Rama.*

One should inculcate devotion with the same intensity of feeling that insects have for light. Kabir Das has gone one step further. He has said that you should be aware of your consciousness with every breath in and out, in such a way that with each breath – and one takes twenty-one thousand six hundred breaths a day – you should only hear So-ham, So-ham, So-ham. If done properly anahad nada will automatically be awakened. Have you read those words of

148

Gorakhnath in which he spoke of the awakening of anahata chakra when one can hear the celestial music.

In a day one takes twenty-one thousand six hundred inhalations and exhalations. We take fifteen breaths a minute normally. An ordinary person may take eighteen a minute, but those who practise meditation have a slower breathing rate. So in an hour there will be nine hundred breaths and in twenty-four hours there will be twenty-one thousand six hundred breaths. This means you have to be conscious of the sound of So Ham with each and every breath. This can be practised only when one is capable of withholding one's urine, stool, hunger and thirst and above all one's sleep – when there are no distractions of any kind. You stop urinating, you stop going to the toilet, you stop eating food, you don't sleep and there are no fluctuations, no distractions of mind. Only then can you be aware of So-ham twenty-one thousand six hundred times in the twenty-four hours.

Such intense concentration is seldom possible. It was possible only for my Bholenath who cared for me twenty-four hours a day. He was the greatest example of a dedicated disciple. He did not leave me even for a moment. He always had his eyes fixed upon me and he never sat with his back to me. If I ever sat behind him then he too would change his position. Some people have told me that an Alsatian has that quality because it is a master's dog. It very much resembles the relationship that a true disciple should have with his guru or master, or a devotee should have with God. Don't you find a similarity between the words 'God' and 'dog'; just reverse the letters and one is altered to the other. What a beautiful relationship between these two words.

The relationship with that dog of mine continued for ten years. I had the feeling that he was special. On the advice of Swami Satsangi, I read a lot of books about dog care. One has to know about bathing, grooming, medicines, vaccinations and so on. Before Bholenath I had no interest in dogs. In fact I was afraid of dogs because as a child that was the message I had received from my parents. We were told that there was a remedy for snakebite but no remedy for

149

dog bite. So initially I was against rearing a dog. I was trapped because of Swami Niranjan.

Early samskaras

Although Bholenath was my dog and stayed by my side twenty-four hours a day, whenever Swami Niranjan was coming from Munger by car, Bholenath would pick up his scent an hour before he reached Rikhia. Bholenath would face north, the direction from which Swami Niranjan was coming, and take deep breaths deeply, as if he had a premonition or could smell his original master. As soon as Swami Niranjan came near me Bholenath would jump up on him and start kissing him from head to foot as if he had just met his long lost friend.

Bholenath was very young when Swami Niranjan left him with me. It is an example of how the *samskaras*, or past impressions, leave a very strong and permanent imprint. When a child is very young and in an innocent state, an imprint planted in the mind becomes permanent. This has an effect on the intellect. But once they become able to understand things, then they are influenced by suggestions, such as not telling lies, and this has an effect. However, during pregnancy, after the *jivatma*, the individual soul, is implanted in the foetus at four months, the education received becomes influential. Everyone should understand this, whether it is the father or mother or servant or any other member of the family. When the child is in the womb, it means that a life force, the jivatma, is there and is capable of being influenced by the surrounding vibrations. No one should forget this. A soul in the mother's womb is much more sensitive than when he is born. He is not aware of anything, he is just a small foetus, but he is very sensitive.

Bholenath was not my dog. I was his foster father. Swami Niranjan's imprint was embedded in the dog's samskaric body at an early age and that feeling appeared when the dog was grown up. That dog knew very well that Swami Niranjan was his master, although Swami Niranjan only used to come here once a month or so. As soon as Bholenath heard the

150

name Niranjan, he would prick up his ears. If he heard me ask Swami Satsangi who was on the phone and she uttered Swami Niranjan's name, Bholenath would immediately get up with his ears cocked. Once I told Swami Satsangi to refer to Swami Niranjan simply as N, but this dog even understood that letter. If I asked who was on the phone and Bholenath heard that it was Swami N, he would be on his feet immediately.

Memories of Bholenath

Bholenath bit many of the swamis here. He could be a vicious dog. One Australian swami's thumb was almost severed from her palm. She was coming towards me when suddenly Bholenath ran after her and by the time I caught hold of him, he had bitten her finger. She subsequently had her finger repaired with microsurgery. Such was the fury of this Bholenath. Even after his death, nobody comes to Ganesha Kutir where presumably his spirit still lingers. Whenever he bit anybody, I would chastise him and then he would prostrate before me. He would beg my forgiveness as if he was saying that he was very sorry for his conduct. But once I excused him, he was his old ferocious self again in a minute.

The day he breathed his last, he just came to me. I was sitting on the chair. He lay down at my feet and he just left his body instantaneously. I never even knew. When I shouted his name, "Bholenath," he was already dead. I asked the sannyasins to remove his body. I have constructed a memorial, a samadhi, for him here out of marble. The epitaph inscribed on Bholenath's samadhi is: "Bholenath: 1990–1999. Companion of Swami Satyananda during his panchagni sadhana." Now, it is for you to decide whether Bholenath was a dog or a man. I never treated him as a dog! I don't believe that he was a dog. He was such a sensitive soul, such a powerful personality, such an example of totality of awareness.

He carried absolutely opposite qualities with him, both lazy and alert, ferocious and loving. If you didn't feed him for one or two days he didn't mind, but if you gave him food he would grab it in two minutes. The man from whom we bought his meat was an ordinary Muslim butcher. He was hardly able to sell one goat a day, but when he started giving meat for Bholenath he became a very successful butcher. Now he has a very big shop and his sons are doing a lot of business. They remember Bholenath and his wife comes and pays homage to Bholenath every year.

The idea of distributing prasad to such a huge gathering came from Bholenath. Everyone who stays here even for a day or two has to help in preparing, stitching, ironing, folding and packing the clothes. Then the packets are labelled so that people get their exact size. This is necessary as these clothes come in huge quantities from all over India and abroad. The whole building is being used for their storage and distribution. This inspiration has come from Bholenath and so the distribution is made in his name. The prasad department started as 'Bholenath's Readymade Store'.

Bholenath and I have the same zodiac sign and birthday. Like me he was born in Dhanurashi, Sagittarius. That dog was a noble soul. He must have been a yogi in his previous birth. He must have done something wrong and hence had to take birth as a dog. This can happen to anyone. All the sannyasins should remember that Bholenath was a sannyasin and a yogi in his previous birth and he used to flirt with women, so he became a dog! That is the genre of dogs. What do you call a person who runs after girls? Don't you call him a dog? Yes, a person with such a demeanour is called a dog.

Prasad – divine blessings
Swami Niranjan: Prasad should be taken as a blessing and not like something you select from a shop. You should not demand a particular item. A blessing like this should be received with reverence. Everybody will get that prasad in some form. Hence each one of you must receive it with due reverence. Only the person whose name is called out should come to receive it, so that nobody misses out. If a person's name is called and a hundred rush to receive, then there is

every likelihood that many might be left out. So, you need only come when I call your name.

Sri Swamiji: There is another point you need to understand so far as the distribution of prasad is concerned. You may have seen monsoon clouds emanating from the sea. Rain falls upon the earth when these clouds are condensed. This rainwater moves to the ocean through rivers and streams and the same process is repeated. The distribution of prasad is like that. Your offerings and Mother Goddess's grace are being distributed. Do not feel that Swamiji obtains all these things by magic. It is not like the deeds of some siddhas or adepts who could manifest butter oil from air or water! These are your gifts that are now being distributed as prasad. You should accept it in that spirit. Just as I did not command you to bring a particular gift, you too should not demand a particular gift. You should not demand a blanket when you are offered a shawl. It is Devi's prasad, so it cannot be your choice. When you go to the market to purchase supplies, you choose the things you like. But when prasad is offered, you have no choice.

However, if a sannyasin gets a sari by mistake or a man gets something usually worn by women or girls, even then you should not bother. Didn't you see me dancing in a sari during the rasalila? You can also dance like that. Why can't grown ups and young people wear a sari? Young people of today mostly dress and live like sariwalis, like ladies. The boys' waists often look smaller than the girls do. A slim waist is generally a trait of sannyasins or girls. The body of a yogi must be slim. The body of a girl should also be slim. But the bodies of sages are very often plump as are the bodies of girls, but lo and behold the sadhu boys are slim! Why then do they feel ashamed of wearing a sari? Oh, I was having a joke with all of you! But it is very true that at times the quinine tablet is administered after mixing it with sweets.

So you must be aware of the prasad. In receiving divine blessings you have no choice. Whatever is offered to you should be accepted as divine grace. The prasad of the yajna is very interesting. The more we distribute, the more there is

153

in stock. All the people of Deoghar district will receive prasad. From the twentieth of December onwards, tractor loads of prasad will go from village to village and each family will be receive prasad in every nook and corner of the area.

Culmination of the yajna

This year is not very cold. The wind is mild and there is a fragrance in the air. The fields are green, mist covers the surrounding fields and you cannot see them clearly. It is just like *avidya*, ignorance, which until removed through knowledge and guru's grace makes everything around you hazy. So, you will have celestial pleasures here tomorrow morning. When dew drops trickle down through the covering over your heads, you will have the feeling that not only is Lord Shiva's *abhisheka*, his ceremonial bath, being done, but that your abhisheka is also being done.

Tomorrow is a very important day and the culmination of the pooja, poornahuti. It is not the termination of the yajna because this is the first year of the Rajasooya Yajna and it will continue next year. So it is the culmination of the yajna. Ramayana Path and kirtan will start at six forty-five and the pooja will begin at seven. I'll be on duty here at six. I know you will be here too. The pooja will be performed from seven to nine. After that there will be worship of the Virgin Marys, the *kanya kumaris*, the young girls, which will take about two hours. We have selected sixty-four girls, some of whom are from Rikhia panchayat and the others are from Harlajori, Deoghar, Bombay, England and America. They will be worshipped, just as you worship the Goddess, fed and given sumptuous gifts.

Oblation to the fire

After that, *poornahuti,* the final oblation to the fire, will be offered on the basis of the four Vedas: the *Rig Veda*, the *Yajur Veda*, the *Sama Veda* and the *Atharva Veda*. May I remind you that when I talk about the Vedas I am not talking about Hinduism. I am talking about the most ancient literature of mankind. The oldest literature in the history of mankind is the literature of the Vedas. It is not religious literature. Literature is never religious, literature is always secular. So on the basis of those four Vedas the oblation to the fire will be offered. Swami Niranjan will create that fire according to the ancient style by friction, through *arani*. Just as the mind comes into friction with an object and an experience is created – objective experience, a perception – in the same way when the mind comes into contact with the symbol Aum, that is also friction. Concentration is also a function, like friction. It is friction between the mind and the yantra or Aum. Then an experience of samadhi, an experience of divine bliss, a transcendental experience takes place. So the fire will be created and there will be oblation. That will take three or four hours.

Gifts for the new brides

After havan we will pay our respects to the newly weds. It is a tradition of this akhara that all the daughters-in-law of this panchayat are honoured on the day when Sita and Rama were married. This is a very important event of this Alakh Bara. We pay our regards to all those daughters-in-law who are here and who have come to this panchayat after their marriage, *dwiragaman*, and we do not do this with empty hands. We offer a compact suitcase containing all the items you offer your daughters when they depart for their in-laws' place. On this auspicious day of the marriage of Sita with Lord Rama, *Vivah Panchami*, we offer gold, silver, pearls, clothes, shoes, ornaments, perfumes, lipstick, hair oil, mirror, comb, soap, vermilion and all the other items comprising the *shringara*, the sixteen items of beautification. We have been offering these things for many years. The number of daughters-in-law varies from year to year; sometimes it is two hundred, sometimes three hundred. One year it swelled to six hundred, but still I did not run out of money! This year, however, there will be about one hundred as for some reason fewer marriages have taken place.

The newly wed girls who have come to my community will be felicitated with dresses, jewellery and many other things, which is a matter of joy for me and which will be a joy for their parents, because each kit will cost about fifty thousand rupees. Sometimes it costs more if you include pure gold. This year I have added a seventeenth item and that is a sanitary towel. So far only sixteen items of beautification have been known to the world. Now I have made it seventeen by adding a sanitary towel. There are intelligent people connected with the ashram and they have sent bundles of sanitary towels.

They have also sent nappies in advance for the expected babies. The newly married couples accept this as a propitious omen with Swamiji's blessings to have healthy and gifted babies. If Swamiji has presented a nappy in advance, the baby must come with high hopes. The idea of diapers was someone else's idea, not mine. Sometimes people crack jokes by offering Huggies, disposal nappies, and diapers, but these simple rural girls are not aware of these things. When the newly weds look at the diaper, they exclaim, "Oh, it is from Poojya Swamiji! That means we will definitely be blessed with a child."

This year someone has also sent good pairs of shoes. I am wearing a pair and they are quite comfortable. The remaining pairs I will present to my sons-in-law. Someone else has presented umbrellas. They will now use umbrellas and raincoats. Next year I will give them gumboots. The female labourers work in the fields transplanting for six or seven hours at a time, standing in mud and water. Some develop sores on their feet. They should be provided with gumboots. In China, Thailand and Japan I have seen women wearing gumboots while working in the fields during the rainy season.

Sita-Rama Vivaha
After the dwiragaman of the daughters-in-laws, the actual wedding ceremony of Sita and Rama will take place, the marriage that took place in Treta Yuga between the daughter of Janaka and the son of Dasharatha. Symbolically they will be represented by Krishna Devi's son and his Sitaji. You are

156

all welcome to participate in that celebration. The bride-groom's party will arrive dancing and jumping to the beating of drums and the playing of other musical instruments. This enclosure is meant for the marriage party who will have to encounter abuse consisting of colourful epithets. The bride's party will not receive abuse but will have to fast on the day of marriage. The bridegroom's party will gleefully swallow all the abuse followed by laddoos and puris.

Swami Niranjan: The abuse will be flavoursome, appetizing and saucy, but the laddoos and puris may upset your digestion.

Sri Swamiji: If you wish to enjoy the abuse then sit here tomorrow. If you happen to go to Barsana you will have to bear with lathis, bamboo sticks, too. We are inviting more and more people to join the bridegroom's party tomorrow so that more and more abuse can be heaped on them. If you are interested in receiving garlands of choice abuse then this enclosure will be the best place for you.

You must all be ready to listen to abuse from the bride's party. The rural womenfolk have come fully prepared. They will say, "This Swamiji does not have a beard." When I had a beard they abused me by complaining, "This Swamiji has a beard." The tone of their abuse has changed now. Swami Niranjan will be abused for being taller. So you must all be ready for that. These maharaj mahanthas from the Agni Akhada in Varanasi and Ananda Akhada will also not be spared. Agni, fire, is hot and ananda is cold. The *Rig Veda* begins with the prayer to the fire, agni. Once this is over you will be free to eat and drink whatever you wish and to sleep as per your own sweet will.

Offerings for Rajasooya Yajna

After the marriage there will be arati and havan which will mark the completion of the yajna for this year. So the first year of the Rajasooya Yajna will be over. Clothes, *vastra daan*, are offered in the first year of a Rajasooya Yajna and in the second year utensils are offered, *patra daan*. So forget about clothes when you come next year. You will be given spoons,

157

pots, thalis, water pots and the like which can be used for eating or in your kitchen. We will offer all the types of utensils that you find in the world.

During the third year of the yajna, it is mandatory to offer food and grains. If it is not done in the third year then it will be done in the fifth year. If it is not done by the fourth or fifth year, then the yajna is considered to be a failure, it becomes null and void. For five days the ashram will feed everybody in and around Rikhia. There will be puri, halwa, laddoos, etc. and if you bring your cows, bullocks, buffaloes, goats, pigs, hens, etc., fodder will be provided for them too during those five days. From sunrise to sunset thousands of people will partake of the food we offer.

This offering of food is called *anna daan*. It is the most difficult part of the yajna. Swami Niranjan told me that he could manage it this year, but I declined because there is a sequence to all these things. Offering of knowledge is of very great importance, greater than the offering of food. Knowledge will be offered in the twelfth year and, God willing, if my mood is conducive, you may have the bliss of shaktipat too from me.

Inspiration from God

Why have we distributed clothing? Gandhi used to tell people that freedom would be achieved only with the strength of a *charkha,* a spinning wheel. Before him, people used to think that freedom could be achieved only through the power of guns, bombs and bullets, through terrorism. But Gandhi was totally opposed to that. He told everyone bluntly that if they became violent, he would stop leading them. He withdrew his non-violent agitation several times. He declared that the spinning wheel should be the main weapon of the freedom struggle. The spinning wheel uses thread, which in Sanskrit is called *sutra*. If taken further, in English sutra means a principle essential for achieving something.

I pondered over it and came to the conclusion that Gandhi's inspiration came from God, because cloth remains with this human body from birth to death – from the cradle

158

to the grave. Everyone has three things – one is his association with God, the second is his prana and the third is this cloth which remains with most of us throughout our lives. So, that very cloth is being given to you as prasad from the Mother Goddess. It would have been easier and cheaper to offer sweets. I could have ordered twenty maunds, eight hundred kilograms, and distributed two pieces each, but if I had distributed a sweet you would have excreted it by tomorrow.

Purpose of yajna – invoking divine grace

This is the first year of the Rajasooya Yajna and it has been going very smoothly. I am sure that the culmination will also be great. It is not a ceremony for amusement or a simple experience. Yajnas are conducted to appeal to Devi to grant us wealth, long life, success, good health and smooth sailing in these disturbed oceans of life. This is the purpose – yajna rectifies life. It is a correcting principle of life. This correction can only be done by a stronger force, not by a human force, but by a divine force.

Life is full of failures, as you know, despondency, guilt and all kinds of other things. The pangs of birth, the pain of being old and then again the pain of rebirth again and again. Everything seems to be full of pain. Ultimately everything ends in depression and disappointment. But there is a power which can set wrong into right. Many of life's calamities can be converted and I am sure that you will all realize this. How nice the yajna was is not important. No! How powerful the yajna was is important. How effective the yajna was is important.

I have always prayed in the sankalpa for the wealth, long life, good health, success and prosperity of everyone. Let everyone be happy, let everyone be healthy, let everyone look upon everyone else with equanimity and may no one ever feel any pain or sorrow. May all be happy, may all be free from disease. May all receive the auspicious blessings of God. May no one experience suffering and if there is suffering then feel happy because God's grace, Mother's grace, the grace of the divine, is in us. The purpose of a yajna is to remove people's pain. There is distress, sorrow and disaster, poverty, disease and fear of death, or death. Many things happen in this earthly life which give us pain and sorrow. This distress can be remedied by divine grace, that is the purpose of this yajna. This is neither a social event nor a spiritual event.

There is a process of formalizing the formless. The Divine Mother's grace is formless and you have to practise rituals to make it tangible and available to all. With this end in view we pray for the well-being of all, for the health and prosperity of all. We also pray that if something has gone wrong, if we have created any muddles, they are sorted out and set right. We invoke Her blessings to protect us from natural calamities, to spread her benign arms to avert impending misfortune. When we feel helpless and our energy and resources are of no avail, then we surrender to the Divine Mother. Yajna is a very effective means of invoking the grace of the Divine Mother. By chanting mantras and by adopting other means, the divine power can be propitiated to descend. We will judge the success of the yajna by sticking to one point.

Has this yajna been successful? Yes, because it has fulfilled some of your desires. The yajna fulfils not only your spiritual desires but your material desires too. Material gain is also God's blessing. Obtaining a good wife or husband, good children, wealth and property is also God's blessing. Nor should any family member fall ill. With this in mind yajnas are performed. In previous years also yajnas have been performed to fulfil this objective. We will be performing yajnas like this in the years ahead. Tomorrow is the concluding day of the yajna. You are all invited to attend, so gird up your loins to sit tight for the whole day to see the marriage.

Life after marriage

Marriage is the most interesting ceremony of life. It is only after marriage that you know what life is. It is like the *peda* or sweet candy of Mathura. Those who taste it repent and

160

those who are deprived of it also repent. Sita used to upbraid Rama at times. That episode is not in the *Ramacharitamanas*, where Tulsidas has depicted Rama as the Godhead, but it is in Valmiki's *Ramayana*. When Sri Rama used to kill the demons, the terrorists of those times, Sita would reprimand him, saying, "Why do you create bad blood?" Rama would reply, "I have decided to exterminate the demons." She would say, "How many will you finish off? One day they will create trouble for you." And one day this happened. Sita was kidnapped by Ravana. Rama became a victim of terrorism.

Although Ravana, the king of the demons, was killed, Ayodhya, Rama's capital, had to suffer the brunt. Valmiki's Sita used to rebuff Rama. His brother Lakshmana also rebuked him. At times Lakshmana would burst into anger. Sita would say, "We will suffer fourteen years of exile in peace and return to Ayodhya after the period of exile is over. Let people suffer, let them fight, what do you want with it?" But Sri Rama was unyielding, saying, "I have taken a vow to rid the earth of the menace of terrorism."

Transcendental marriage
The marriage of Sita and Rama takes place in various dimensions. One dimension is the one you will see tomorrow between a man and a woman. A wedding is one dimension of marriage. But there is another dimension where the spirit joins the higher transcendental experience. The mind is wedded to the self, the mind is wedded to the spirit. I don't know when that marriage will take place.

Rama represents the indweller of all beings. Rama is the all-pervading, ever-permeating, omnipresent reality and Sita is the spirit. God is not alone. God has a power within Him and that power is called Sita. There are many people who think that God is alone, that he is a bachelor. My God is not a bachelor. If we were to ask if the gods have consorts, we would find that Rama has Sita, Vishnu has Lakshmi, Brahma has Saraswati and Shiva has Parvati.

161

Satsang 15

December 19, 2001

*Y*ajna is the basis of Indian culture. In ancient times, yajnas were performed all over the world. I have travelled extensively in southern Colombia. Where there is a large stretch of dense forest, called Sant Augustine. At different places there are stone statues and from those relics we know that the ancient tribes used to perform fire ceremonies. However, with the passage of time everything was lost. In India the tradition was maintained. Various forms of yajnas were performed in this country by kings and emperors. When yajna is performed by an individual, it is called havan. You can practise it at home also. Many members of Arya Samaj do havan once a week in their homes. But I am talking about yajna, not havan. Yajna is a colossal event in India. There are many aspects of yajna; it is not only the ritual, the pooja. Ordinary people cannot perform yajna.

There is documentation that in Treta Yuga Rama performed the Rajasooya Yajna for a period of twelve years. He built an entirely new yajna complex outside Ayodhya where many great sages and saints like Yajnavalkya, Chyavanarishi, Bharadvaja and Vishwamitra attended. Rama went to Agastya personally to invite him, because Agastya was intensely involved in the Rama-Ravana episode. It was Agastya who helped Sri Rama to rescue Sita.

In Dwapara Yuga Yudhishthira performed another Rajasooya Yajna. When Duryodhana and his father Dhritarashtra would not agree to share the empire with the Pandavas, they gave them a place called Indraprastha. You know the story. A city was built in Indraprastha and Yudhishthira conducted the Rajasooya Yajna there. In that particular yajna the most important person was Sri Krishna, who attended as a VIP. He washed the feet of every guest and removed the leaf plates after people had finished eating. That was Sri Krishna's duty and it is documented in the *Mahabharata*. It was during that Rajasooya Yajna that Draupadi made the pungent remark, "A blind man's son is also blind."

The Rajasooya Yajna can only be conducted by someone who is a conqueror, who has established his sovereignty everywhere. It is not performed on the strength of wealth or manpower, nor on the strength of a royal sceptre. Only one who has swept the globe is entitled to undertake the Rajasooya Yajna. Flags and banners are of various types. When one nation has complete sway over the world, that is political supremacy. I have also established my sway and supremacy over the world, but it is of a different kind. Mine is the banner of yoga that is fluttering in every island, every city and every important place. Yoga has been accepted by all communities and all religious groups.

Christ in India

When I met the Pope at the Vatican, he asked me how I would fit yoga, an oriental philosophy, with an occidental culture. He was speechless when I told him that Christianity was an oriental philosophy. Christ lived in India for twelve years – and the Pope asked me how an oriental science would fit with occidental culture! Christ was not a European, Christ was a Jew. Christ was not a Christian, Christ was not a Protestant or a Catholic. Christianity is an oriental philosophy. Two thousand years ago a great man was born in the orient. His name was Jesus Christ. Most of you know the story. Near Christ's birthplace there was a monastery

163

belonging to the Essene sect. Fifty years before Christ was born that had monastery closed, but five years before his birth it began functioning again.

Jesus was the son of a carpenter named Joseph. His mother's name was Mary; we call her Mariam. One night Joseph had a dream that Jesus had been born from Mary's womb without any sexual interaction having occurred. Ordinary people are born as a result of sexual interaction. But there are exceptions. Sri Rama was immaculate. We call such people incarnations of God. They are the effulgence of divinity, they are personifications of divinity. The divine light entered into a woman's womb and a son was born – Rama, or Krishna, or Christ.

Christ was immaculate like Sri Rama and Sri Krishna. Sri Rama was not born as a result of sexual interaction between Dasharatha and Kaushalya. Rama was born after Dasharatha performed the Putresthi Yajna in Ayodhya. Rishi Shringi conducted that yajna, as a result of which Sri Rama, Lakshmana, Bharata and Shatrughna were born. So when you say 'incarnation of God' you mean that the child was born without sexual interaction between a man and a woman. That is how Christ was born.

Christ was not a European, he was a Jew. Buddha was not a Buddhist, he was a Hindu. Mahavir was not a Jain, he was a Hindu. I have studied history. I have studied Persian and Arabic. I have studied the Koran and the Hadith. I am a Hindu sannyasin. I have read the Bible many times. I have read all the bibles, oriental and otherwise. Knowledge is always beyond religion, beyond sex, beyond nationality, beyond civilization, beyond history. Knowledge is knowledge. Learn everything. Don't say, "I am a Hindu, I won't read the Bible." Don't say, "I am a Muslim I won't read the Gita." No, if the Bible has knowledge have it! If the Koran has knowledge have it!

Just as the philosophy of Christ was given to Europeans, similarly I gave yoga to Europeans. I did not do anything unusual. The spirit of Christ, the teachings of Christ, the knowledge and the message that he gave emerged from

Varanasi. Christ spent time in Varanasi, in Kathmandu, in Puri. He spent time in Chennai, in southern India,. There are written archives, but they are a part of history you will never be taught. We are not taught the right history, we are taught the history which is recognized and stamped by the ruling clan for their own political gain. This is the truth. What harm is there in saying that Christ lived in India? Why shouldn't we get the credit for having a great man on our soil. I am talking to the church. Why don't you give us the honour of having a great man, an historical personality, in our country? After all, geographically the world is one. Nationally, India is India, Italy is Italy, Germany is Germany, but geographically it is one earth. We have divided it.

Mantra initiation

After meeting with the Pope I went to South America. Whenever I visited the South American countries people would ask for mantra diksha. I started initiating them into the sannyasa fold by giving them mantras. Aspirants would queue in large numbers up to three kilometres long and it was hard to deal with such big groups. So I designed a formula and appointed a secretary to process the applications. The aspirants were required to furnish some essential information such as their *rashi*, or zodiac sign, and *lagna*, or the sun's entrance into a zodiac sign, so that their mantra could be selected on the basis of the element predominant in their personality. If a person is born in Dhanurashi, the ninth sign of the zodiac, the element of fire is predominant. If the element of water is predominant then the mantra is decided after taking that into consideration. If the ether element is predominant then the mantra will change. Taking these astrological points into consideration, I designed a system to facilitate selection of the appropriate mantra.

In India the system followed is quite different. The mantra is decided on the basis of your faith and reverence for the deity. If you are a devotee of Lord Shiva then the mantra would be 'Om Namah Shivaya' and if one is a devotee of Sri Rama then the mantra would be 'Sri Rama Jai Rama

165

Jai Jai Rama'. In Vedic culture the mantra is decided on the basis of the astrological calculation. However, Christians and others do not have horoscopes and so a different system has to be designed for them.

The number of aspirants was so high that we would work out the details at night so that the initiations would be speeded up during the daytime. I would give the Spanish version of the Sanskrit mantra to the South American aspirants. I would also give them malas and instructions in how to count the beads. In my evening lectures I would explain how to repeat the mantra in japa form. Whoever came to take diksha gave dakshina generously.

Spirituality and Westerners

In South America the devotees go to church, light a candle and bow their heads. I went to the churches and spread the message of yoga. The church leaders came to see me and serve me. I gave them geru and spiritual names. They accepted and recognized me as a yoga guru from India. The flag of yoga started fluttering over South America. I had complete and unchallenged sway there. I repeat once again that victory is not achieved only by the sword. There was a time when the sword was the most powerful weapon. Kings and chieftains used to establish their political supremacy on the strength of the sword. But Swami Vivekananda never used a sword and he registered his spiritual supremacy over the Western world. Adi Shankara also established spiritual supremacy without using weapons.

Only a magician has the power to hypnotize the people but the art of magic is not unreal. What you see is not actually there. But I was a different type of magician. I hypnotized the people by giving them something tangible. What is digvijaya? To hold sway everywhere amounts to wielding territorial power over a vast area. But in the present context sovereign power means the dominating of spiritual culture.

People from Western countries wallow in wealth; they possess huge material wealth, they have scientific knowledge and are well-equipped in all spheres of life. They are satiated;

166

they have enough of everything. They are fully employed and don't suffer from material want. In every respect they are affluent people, they have an excess of everything. They have nothing to worry about. Then what do they do? After excessive material enjoyment they develop distaste for it all. Spiritual thoughts preoccupy their minds. Western people had become allergic to worldly enjoyments and were in dire need of something higher. They were in search of an alternative source of enjoyment. I understood their problem and took up the cudgels. I undertook the task of teaching spirituality to Westerners and my efforts were successful.

Spirit of sannyasa

The great Buddha died leaving behind ten thousand disciples. A band of ten thousand *bhikshus* or monks was ready long before he gave up the ghost. My sannyasin disciples are sitting here in large numbers. I have allowed some relaxation in the sannyasa code. I am in favour of constitutional amendment. From time to time there should be some amendments to suit the changing times. There should not be any rigidity in the constitution of a nation nor in the constitution of the sannyasa order. There should be flexibility everywhere.

The basic spirit of sannyasa is trusteeship. This means that I am not the owner of this property, I am not the proprietor of anything, I am just a trustee. A sannyasin should have no attachment of any kind. Nothing belongs to a sannyasin. He has no wife, no children, no household, no bank balance, no property. Even this body is not mine. This prana is not mine. The ashram is not mine. The money is not mine. Nothing belongs to me. The basic spirit of sannyasa is no *mamata*, no sense of ownership. The basic spirit of a sannyasin is to have no attachments whatsoever. Where there is no attachment, there in no infatuation. Where there is mamata, there has to be maya. There has to be *moha*, delusion, and *avidya*, ignorance. But when you don't have mamata there is no maya, no moha, no delusion, no mineness, no self-interest and no ignorance. When nothing

167

belongs to me there is knowledge and knowledge and knowledge.

The mainstay of sannyasa is sacrifice and renunciation. Sannyasins of different sects wear different types of clothes, some don geru, some put on black, others dress in yellow and yet others wear white. It doesn't make any difference. In India, Vaishnavas wear quite different clothing to Shaktas. Sannyasins who have given up everything do not necessarily wear only geru but put on different colours. Some grow matted hair, some have their heads shaved. The sannyasins of Juna Akhara smoke chillums. They enjoy a puff on the chillum and justify it by saying it is a sign of masculinity. But we do not smoke, nor do we indulge in passive smoking. Smoking is not at all essential in sannyasa. The essential ingredient of sannyasa is sacrifice. I have always emphasized this element of sannyasa.

Oceans of knowledge

There are many talented ones in my sannyasa order, scientists and technologists who are consulted by their respective governments and research organizations. Some are experts on satellite technology and information technology. A few are experts on armament technology too. They create miracles of science. They work in companies on a contract basis for six or nine months, earn a lot of money and return to the ashrams. They participate in our activities and help in the running of the ashrams.

What I wish to emphasize is that sannyasins should not be illiterate. A sannyasin should be an ocean of knowledge. I know the constitution of India by heart. I can tell you all the amendments that have been made to the Indian constitution. I know all about criminal law, administrative and judicial law. I know how the CBI works. We are not illiterate or uneducated sadhus, ignoramuses or nincompoops. My sannyasins are knowledgeable and accomplished and competent enough to run establishments. To don geru and have one's head shaved is not the qualification of a sadhu. He has to be a fully qualified person.

168

We run many establishments. We have a big establishment in Australia. My sannyasins are spread all over the world. They have all set up small temples of their own and given them names such as Yogashram, Yoga Institute, Yoga Academy, School of Yoga, Yoga Centre etc. Yoga centres are our temples. Yoga means union. Union of what? The union of ida and pingala in sushumna. The temples in India are symbols of this ida, pingala, sushumna and the devata inside is the spirit, the Shiva, the Vishnu, the Ganesha, or Devi or anything else.

Although we give them different names – Rama, Krishna, Devi, Durga – we don't understand them differently. For us Rama is equal to Krishna is equal to Shiva is equal to Ganesha is equal to Devi. All are equal to each other. There is no difference. Water is water, whether it is in a well or a pond or a drum or a bottle. Water is water. All the devatas are equal to each other. Whether you call Him Rama or Rahim or Krishna, the meaning is the same. Whether you call it soap or *sabun*, water or *pani*, the meaning is the same. We see difference in the terminology, we see difference in understanding, but we do not see any difference in the basics.

Polytheistic societies
We worship the embodied deity. We are not monotheistic because monotheism brings disaster to society. All the world's terrorists are monotheists. Monotheistic philosophy breeds intolerance and ultimately it reflects in your political system. The impact of philosophy on a political system is felt in times to come. To have a better society, to have a non-violent society, to have a society with greater understanding and better tolerance, you should always have a polytheistic society. Polytheism always has a positive impact on a nation's politics, culture and civilization. On the other hand, the impact of monotheism has an adverse impact. Therefore, in Indian philosophy, although the Upanishads speak of one God, they add that this God has various forms: *Ekam sat viprah bahudha vadanti* – "Though Truth of the Supreme Spirit is one, the wise identify Him by various names."

169

It is therefore not necessary to worship one God alone, as there are various forms of God. It is also foolish to say that God is without form. God is both without form, *nirakara*, and with form, *sakara*. It is up to you to make a choice about how to worship Him, to adore Him and to ask a boon from Him. You have to make a choice between the formless God and the embodied God and offer your obeisance to Him. You are absolutely free to exercise your preference for any form of God. Hanuman is not greater than Sri Rama and Sri Rama is not superior to Hanuman. Even so Devi is not superior to Sri Krishna and likewise Sri Krishna is not greater than Devi. Take another example. Previously I had one name, now I have another name, but I remain the same. Can you say which of my two names is greater? The names may be different, but the ultimate truth is the same.

Many paths to salvation

I explained all these things to the Westerners. I told them that their forefathers were polytheists, that two thousand years ago their forefathers had been forced to accept monotheism. I explained to them that the Anglo Saxons had a polytheistic culture. The forefathers of the Americans, English and Australians were polytheistic. I can accept any challenge you may have on this score. Their ancestors were polytheistic and worshipped various deities. Two thousand years ago they were forced to accept monotheism, or otherwise they were burnt alive.

I do believe that Christianity is one way to salvation, but it is wrong to say that Christianity is the only way to salvation. My house has more than one door. If you are coming to Deoghar it is not essential to go via Bhagalpur. You can come via Calcutta; you are free to take the route through Kathmandu or Mumbai to reach Deoghar. There are many doors to my house. You may enter through any of them. I have hammered this idea into people's minds – that God is not one. God is infinite. God is an integral whole.

What does infinite mean? It means complete and whole, absolute and total. It is incorrect to say that God is one.

170

When you say God is one, then you say He is not two, He is not three. One is a mathematical number. I don't talk about God in terms of mathematics. I talk about God in terms of philosophy. God is infinite. Infinity contains one plus, plus, plus, plus – infinity. When you say that God is one, you are not making a mathematical statement, you are saying God is full, whole, pervasive. Infinity means, *Poornamadah poornamidam poornaat poornamudachyate poornasya poornamaadaaya poornamevaavashishyate.* God is absolute and indivisible. That is full, this is full, and from that full emerges this full. *Poorna* means all that is there, everything.

The formless God which we were talking about is also infinite and the embodied form of God is also infinite. Devi, Durga, Kali, A, B, C, D, whatever name you remember the supreme spirit by, is infinite, full. Even if you remove something from that fullness, it will still remain full. Even if you do not accept the formless God you will not lose anything. Even if you say that God is not formless, He is in an embodied form, He is sitting in Baidyanath temple, He is in the Pashupatinath temple in Kathmandu, He is in the Jagannath temple in Puri, you are not off the mark. The concept of infinity, of fullness, is like this. Just as water, air, oxygen and light are present everywhere, so God is present everywhere. Therefore, God should not really be conceived as formless. To say that God is formless is not correct. God is not at all formless. The entire creation is His form. The entire universe is His manifestation. The ocean, the mountains, the trees, the sky, the sun and the moon are His forms. I am His form, you are His form. This is reality.

God's instrument

We were talking about the Rajasooya Yajna. I am a digvijayi, a victor of the universe, for God has made me His instrument. I am a very ordinary person. I was born in a village and brought up in simple circumstances. Although my family owned a lot of agricultural land I wore the same old shoes and tattered clothes as the villagers usually do. I came from that rural background. I used to read by the dim light of a kerosene lamp and look after the cattle during the day. Such was my life in the village.

When I entered my guru's ashram I had to wash and clean the large cooking vessels although I was still a young boy of diminutive height. Even today I am a man of diminutive size. In order to clean the bottoms of the vessels I had to climb into them and as a result my whole body would be covered with black soot. I also had to dig through the hard rock of a hill to construct a water channel to the ashram. Remember the story of Majnu and Laila? Majnu, the celebrated lover of Laila, spent the whole night digging through rock in order to have a glimpse of his beloved. While he was digging, Majnu cried out, "Laila, Laila, Laila." Following in his footsteps I also cried out, "Gurudev, Gurudev, Gurudev," while digging the channel. When I had completed the task, I built a huge water tank in the ashram for water storage. Then we started constructing buildings on the ashram premises. There is nothing I did not do in my guru's ashram.

Frankly speaking, I have not read the yogic scriptures, I have not read any books on yoga, but I have written many books on yoga which are so authentic that nobody has ever found fault with them. Yoga was not my discipline. I am a sannyasin. I belong to the order of sannyasa established by Adi Shankaracharya. You may read *Panchadashi* and *Viveka-chudamani* to learn more about my sannyasa order. I am not a *vairagi*, a recluse. I am not a *udasi*, a hermit. I am a sannyasin of the Dashnami order of sannyasa established by Adi Shankara. Saraswati, Giri, Parvata, Sagara, Vanam, Aranya, Ashrama, Tirtha, Puri and Bharati are sub-sects of the Dashnami tradition. As you know I am a Saraswati sannyasin of the Dashnami tradition and my subject is Vedanta, which is based on the Upanishads. In Vedanta the mantra is Soham. The terms *pooraka*, inhalation, or *rechaka*, exhalation, are not used. When you repeat 'Soham' it becomes pranayama. When you think of Brahma it becomes *kumbhaka*, retention. When your mind stops it becomes kumbhaka. When your mind wanders it becomes rechaka, exhalation.

I used to talk like this, but things took a different turn when my guru asked me to teach yoga. I didn't know yoga, but I taught yoga and wrote many books on yoga, which have sold well. When I read my own books now I am amazed and ask myself, "Satyananda, where did you learn all this? How did you know that there are seventy-two thousand nadis? You never studied that subject. Where did you learn it all?" Now I feel that there was someone sitting inside me who was speaking through me and who did all the writing.

Who wrote *Ramacharitamanas*, for example? They say there were a number of learned people like Tulsidas in the world, great Sanskrit scholars, but nobody could wield such a pen. How could Tulsidas compose such a great epic of the stature of the *Ramacharitamanas*? Maybe sitting inside Tulsidas' human frame was *paramatma*, the supreme soul, or *divyashakti*, the divine power, or Goddess Saraswati and He or She dictated the epic using Tulsidas as an instrument. I too was made an instrument by that divine power in order to write so many books on yoga and tantra. Works of eternal value are called *shruti*, revealed truth. The Vedas are shruti, *Ramacharitamanas* is shruti. Christians accept the Bible as shruti, a revelation. The Muslims treat the Koran as shruti. Shruti means the voice of God.

Prasad of the Rajasooya Yajna

This is the first year of the Rajasooya Yajna. In the first year clothes are given as prasad and in the second year utensils and vessels will be distributed. In the third year we will give cooked food as prasad. One day you will get gold and silver as prasad. It is not a big thing. It is you who offer it all. Yes, you are the donors. Some of you may get diamond rings, some gold. We may cover one thousand, ten thousand, twenty thousand, thirty thousand people. Everyone here will receive prasad because you are the people who contribute it.

As is the practice, when kings and emperors come to attend the Rajasooya Yajna they offer diamonds, gold, emeralds, sapphires, pearls and so on to the *chakravarti samrat*, the great monarch, and the monarch distributes it as

173

prasad to the people. The chakravarti receives it as a gift or offering and gives it away as the prasad of the yajna. In ancient times the Rajasooya Yajna was performed on a very large scale. We are following the same tradition. Even today many yajnas are held in this country compared to which this is a miniature yajna. But this is a prelude to a very major event. We believe in that rich tradition. My Indian guests and disciples must keep that in mind.

Changing role of sannyasins in society

Although the government is run by the government machinery, the progress of the country can't be assured by the government. For the development of the nation and society, self-governing institutions and organizations should emerge. This country lacks such institutions. Institutions dedicated to welfare and development are very few in this country. We have to depend on the government for education, defence and protection, water, grain, hospitals and many other things. This system is wrong and needs to change.

Too much dependence on government leads to many ills. It gives birth to social maladies. To develop the country we require institutions of a different kind to run the country. We require institutions that can cater to the needs of society. Every society can ensure its own security and meet its own needs. This is a vision, a utopia which may take concrete shape in the course of time.

I talk openly to spiritual leaders, scholars and intellectuals and give them my suggestions. I ask the sadhus to adopt or to take charge of a panchayat and the development of the villages. If each sadhu were to adopt one panchayat and put his heart and soul into the all round development of the area, it would not even take five years to see the results. If every sannyasin were to take up the regeneration of one panchayat he would not lack the resources to execute his mission. Sannyasins are very resourceful members of this country. This is nothing new, you all know that.

There is another point I have to make. If it is not essential for you to enter householder life, then you should not do so.

174

Live like us – alakh niranjan. Exactly like us. This suggestion must be carried out because a sannyasin is capable of doing what no one else in this country can do. A sannyasin cannot ignore his duties. But most sannyasins today are not able to keep up with the changing times. I am not criticizing anyone or passing any judgement. The main aim of a sannyasin is to impart knowledge. However, in view of the emerging situation, sannyasins have to divert their attention from the written code to the betterment of humanity. They will have to open hospitals, colleges or other institutions. This is not the duty of a sannyasin, it is your duty. But as you have failed miserably to do it, and do not have the time or money beyond what you do for your own sons and daughters, it will have to be done by the sannyasins.

The situation that has developed is not the fault of the sannyasins. The culture of this country is alive because of the sannyasins. Although it is not the domain of sannyasins they will have to shoulder the dual responsibility of educating people and keeping our ancient religion and culture alive. I do not blame the sannyasins for the ills of this country, but since they are the only ones with the will and the resources at their command, I call upon them to undertake this yeoman duty.

Furthermore, those who do not have the urge for family life should undertake a new life for a few years at least, sacrifice their youth and join one of the ashrams – Aurobindo Ashram, Ramakrishna Mission, Sivananda Ashram or Kanchi Peeth Ashram. There are many such ashrams in India where you can take sannyasa and obtain knowledge. In this way you too will gain resources and then you can take up a panchayat and uplift the downtrodden and the deprived.

You have to develop strong institutions, not religious institutions. You can open and run homes for the destitute. Many people have opened hospitals for lepers which are providing very good services. Many have opened libraries. Satya Sai Baba, Mother Amritananda, the saints of Kanchi Kamkoti Peetham, the sannyasins of Ramakrishna Mission and other spiritual institutions have opened hospitals,

175

colleges and other institutions for the well-being of people. Swami Sivananda's disciples also run several such institutions. Now the sannyasins will have to widen their area of operation and shoulder the responsibility of the nation.

A spiritual land

This is not a country of traders, although they are also a part of this country, but a country of teachers, gurus and preceptors. If anyone is to become a preceptor, a guru, then he will not look towards China, Japan, Russia, Argentina or England. He must look towards India to become a real guru. Have you ever found a person who aspired to be a guru and went to America? No. The manufacturing unit lies here in India! If someone wants to earn dollars, then he will go to America. That is why we find men and women from this country adopting Western clothes and proceeding to the West and the USA, but those in the West who want to acquire spiritual knowledge change over to a dhoti and kurta, shave their heads and come to India.

India is a country of gurus and it has been watered by the great rivers of this land – the Ganga, Yamuna, Saraswati, Kaveri and many others. There are innumerable pilgrim places, *tirthas*, from north to south India. Every state has such tirthas. Every province has many ashrams. There are twelve jyotirlingas and fifty-two shaktipeethas in this land of ours. We have sixty-four yoginipeethas too. You will find all that you aspire for there. Where else will you go then? You can find discotheques anywhere if that is what you want, but you cannot find spirituality anywhere else except in this country. This land of great seers is a spiritual land. All those who aspired for knowledge and realization came here.

Influence of Vaishnavism and Buddhism on Christianity

Even Christ came to India. As a child Christ used to question the leaders of the Essene community and they gave him whatever knowledge they had. However, they were not able to answer all his questions on spirituality. They told him that there were many questions which only the Indian seers

176

could answer. Christ came to India by the overland route. He travelled all over India and took with him the philosophy that was prevalent here two thousand years ago.

In those days Vaishnavism and Buddhism were prevalent here. What you find in Christianity today is an amalgam of bhakti and raja yoga from the Vaishnava tradition and the universality of Buddhism. In Christianity you find the yamas and niyamas – *satya* (truth), *ahimsa* (non-violence), *asteya* (non-stealing), *aparigraha* (non-accumulation), *shaucha* (cleanliness), *brahmacharya* (celibacy). That is raja yoga. How then can you differentiate between raja yoga and Christianity? Raja yoga is one of the most important components of Christianity. What is bhakti? God you are everything. I am Thine, My Lord, Let Thy will be done – that is Vaishnava bhakti.

So Christianity can easily be said to be a confluence of raja yoga and bhakti yoga. When Christ came to India at that time these two cultures, Buddhism and Vaishnavism, were flourishing here. In Buddhism there is *achara*, good behaviour, and *vichara*, reflection, which are rules of conduct. In Vaishnavism there is bhakti, bhakti and bhakti – total surrender to God. Vaishnavism is bhakti. Buddhism is a way of living. Christ took these two philosophies with him and their amalgam was known subsequently as Christianity.

Remember that Christ came to India twice. Christ breathed his last in India. In the same way as Buddha acquired realization at Gaya, Christ achieved realization in India and left his mortal body here. Christ did not die on the cross; there is no proof. Christ died in Kashmir, in India. Christ was crucified, but did not die because he was a yogi. He was treated and cured and then he lived and preached surreptitiously in what is now Iraq.

He came to India about thirteen years after his crucifixion, at which time he was already about forty-nine or fifty years of age. His mother Mary and another companion named Magdalene came with him. Mary has a *mazar*, a tomb, in Srinagar. It still exists and is called the grave of Mariam. It is near Hazrat Bal in Kashmir where the sacred hair of the prophet is kept. Outside Hazrat Bal, there is a tomb named Nabi Asaf. It is also called the tomb of Yuz Asaf. The keeper of the tomb is a Muslim. I have been there. Many tourists go there. One of my disciples offered a payment to the keeper of the tomb if he would show him the records relating to the tomb, but the keeper would not permit it and refused to part with the records.

This is not something that history has said. It is as I say it. This is what has happened and what has happened need not be a part of history. History is written for a purpose. Many things are concealed, many things are added, many things are bloated, many things are floated and many things are destroyed. The history that you read has been dictated. It is not the real history of what happened. There are many entries that happened and many more that did not occur.

But Christ was buried here in Kashmir. There is a reference, an *aayat*, in the Koran to this. It is written clearly, "So did we bury Yesu the Nabi, the son of Mary, in the land of rivers, rivulets, waterfalls, valleys, forests and meadows." *Nabi* means prophet. We call him Yesu, like you say Jesus. In Spanish it is Isus and the 'I' is pronounced 'ya'. So Yesu the Nabi, the son of Mary or Mariam, was buried in the land of valleys, forests, meadows, rivers, rivulets and waterfalls.

Israel has no answer to this description. Only Kashmir has the meaning. We are proud that Christ came to our country and we are proud that he died here. Maybe one day we will also have a temple for Christ, like we have mandirs for Chandi, Devi, Durga, Rama, Krishna and Hanuman. He will become one of our gods. Why not? Let God come in many forms. Let God come in thousands of forms. Just as you want many models of shoes, clothes, telephones and cars, so let there be hundreds of models of God also. Choose any one. Some have chosen Christ – okay; some have chosen Hanuman – good; some have chosen Devi – perfect!

Assimilating all religions
While speaking about the Rajasooya Yajna, I digressed slightly to tell you something else which was not without a purpose.

Our digestive system should be strong enough to digest all the other philosophies of the world. We have to assimilate them. We have done it in the past when many sects, thoughts and religions were assimilated into our religion, and yet our own Sanatan Dharma remained intact. You cannot destroy a religion. Don't have such wishful thinking. All religions – Christianity or Islam or Buddhism – are products of a supermind. Politicians misuse them, as you well know, but just because religions are misused by politicians we should never think negatively about a religion. We should be able to metabolize it. Religion is also metabolized like the food you eat and digest. Our seers and saints gave us the strength and the art of assimilating them and yet keeping our own dharma intact.

Your rishis and munis, your wise men, have given you permission to follow any religion, to talk about any religion, to believe in any religion. Your ancestors gave you full permission to worship in any form. Nobody can say, "Why do you read the Bible?" Why not? It is your right. Your ancestors said you can read the Bible and worship God in any shape or form. There is nothing to be afraid of. If you practise that, you should be able to digest all types of food one day. Haven't you seen that I have been able to digest and assimilate the Shaktas, the Vaishnavas, the Shaivas, the followers of Hanuman and Kali, the Jains, the Buddhists, the Pashupats, the Christians and some of the Muslims too. Yogis have the capacity to unite and assimilate all sects and religions and this is the definition of a digvijayi. This is the way. Why has your digestive system become so weak?

Rama had that power. That is described in the *Ramacharitamanas*. There were many castes, sects and creeds in his age. There were men and women of innumerable faiths. The number of religious sects was great. He assimilated each one of them. How did he do it? Not by the sword, of course! You cannot metabolize religions with a crusade or jihad. They are not the right methods. Jihad and crusade are political acts. That is not the correct way to have faith in every religion, to follow the dictums of every religion. The

179

right approach is to recognize the philosopher or prophet of every religion. No jihad and no crusade. I don't say that my way is the only way. No. My way is one of the ways. I never say that my path is the only path. What I propose is that it is one of the paths. This is the message that should he communicated to the world at large.

Colombia

When I was in Colombia, the number of initiates was more than two thousand and the queue for initiations was so long that people were there from dawn to dusk. Everyone in the queue was given a piece of paper with their initiation details and when their turn came they would kiss my hand. No matter how I cautioned them not to, they would always kiss my hand after initiation. Once I told one such disciple that he should take care lest my hand would vanish! Have you seen the lingam at Baidyanath Dham? People rubbed their palms on the lingam and ultimately it was worn down to ground level. It has been almost rubbed away. So I thought that a similar fate awaited me in Colombia. I could not imagine why they loved kissing hands, as it seemed to me a most unhygienic habit.

However, the Colombians and most South Americans are by and large very noble and simple people. They are of Spanish origin, having gone there during the sojourn of Columbus and finally settled there. Later they were assimilated with the local tribes who were the natives of Colombia. Originally Incas, Aztecs and Chibchas resided in South America and these tribes used to worship the sun. In those days women and girls dressed in white robes and performed the priestly duties in the sun temples.

When the Spanish went there after Columbus, they plundered the nation and criminally assaulted the native tribes. But ultimately these invaders had to make peace with the local tribes. They had not gone with their families and hence as soldiers they married the locals and settled there. The present generation is the progeny of this cross between the two. Most people in South America are not pure Spanish;

180

they are completely mixed now. Thus the new generation has traits of the original tribes and of the Spanish culture, like the song from the Indian film 'Awara',

Mera jhoota hai Japani, yeh patloon Englishtani,
sar pe lal topi Russi phir bhi dil hai Hindustani.

"My shoes are Japanese, these pants are English, on my head is a red Russian cap, but my heart is still Indian."

Iran

Many years ago I went to Baghdad, the capital of Iraq. Saddam Hussein was the ruler. My disciples celebrated Guru Poornima there and gave me a lot of offerings. At that time the economic situation in Iraq was very good. In 1968 I visited Iran too as the guest of honour of the Shah. I was treated like a prince and asked to speak on television for ten or fifteen minutes. After the program was over the viewers were asked if they had any questions. The questions were mostly on kundalini, chakras, nadis, lokas, mantra, shaktipat, samadhi, etc. The way the people in Iran asked questions I thought that I was in India. I am talking about the similarity of culture.

I had had experience of television programs elsewhere when most of the questions asked were clumsy, but in Iran the questions were clear and specific. When someone asks a question it should be intelligible, but in most places it was hard to make head or tail of them. Once I was asked why I hadn't married. Now, isn't that a shameless question to ask a sannyasin? What could I say?

Holy cow

One person in England asked why the cow in India is treated as holy. I lost my cool and retorted, "You carry dogs in your car and in India a bullock pulls a cart. You kiss your dogs, but in India although we do not kiss the cow, we revere them as they give us milk. Our cow is beneficial to us and your dogs are not beneficial to you. You love dogs, I love cows. Your dog is a holy dog. My cow is a holy cow. It's my

181

right to worship a cow. Even as it is your right to kiss a dog, it is my right to worship a cow! How dare you ask me this question."

That day I was very angry. I had never questioned why people keep dogs, but they dared to joke about why we keep cows. Those cows give us milk and compost. Of all the waste products in the world only cow's dung is sacred. All other types of wastes, whether industrial, nuclear, human or animal, are harmful. Only cow's dung is virus free, safe and beneficial. If you know of any other waste in the world that is as good, then tell me. Stupid questions are asked about such a pious animal! Many other strange questions have been put to me, but not the questions asked in Iran.

I went to Iran twice on a ticket from New York–Teheran–New York–Teheran. The people in Teheran were very happy with me. They invited me to dinner after my last program. I politely refused and told them that they ate beef and a sannyasin like me did not eat non-vegetarian food, especially beef. For us the cow is the holiest of all creatures. We consider the cow to be holier than God. We treat cows as being holier than our deities. The Iranians were perplexed and asked me what they should offer me at the proposed feast. At that time there were two Sikh gurudwaras in Teheran, one old and the other new. I was staying in the new gurudwara. These Sikh brothers had started a *langar*, free meals for all, in the gurudwara. Loaves, tarka, a concoction of pulse, and halwa were served and these three dishes satisfied us all.

The Iranian Defence Minister also participated in that dinner. When I arrived they all stood up and said something in Persian, which I could not follow. I could follow the last address, however, which was *noukram-chaakram*, meaning they were my servants. Then they asked me to begin eating. So, I remember those people and their country very much.

Sufism

The Iranian culture is derived from Sufism, which combines both devotion and yoga. Sufi culture and philosophy is a confluence of prema bhakti and raja yoga samadhi. It is pure bhakti. But not *ghanti-vanti wala bhakti*, not simply the bell ringing type of devotion. *Prema bhakti* is where you love God, that line of devotion in which the person praying treats himself as the beloved and God as the lover. The boy is *ashique*, the lover, and the girl is *mashuque,* the beloved. What do you understand by love? Sufis call it *ishq,* which means love – love of anything. Loving your child is ishq. Loving a girl is ishq. Loving a man is ishq. Loving God is ishq. But there is a difference between the two. One is ishq haqiqi and the other is ishq mijazi. *Ishq haqiqi* means divine love. *Ishq mijazi* is worldly love. Divine love is bhakti and worldly love is maya. This is the basis of Sufism, which is very prevalent in Iran. They sing and dance very well, which are forms of devotion.

Music and dance – the elixir of life

In Indian culture, Shiva is the master of dance, the beautiful dancer, loved by all – *Nataraja Nataraja nartan sundar Nataraja. Shivaraja Shivaraja Shivakami priya Nataraja.* Once Shiva and Parvati were having a dance competition. He would give a performance and she would follow. Shiva and Parvati danced and danced and danced. Shiva danced in different poses and ultimately he adopted a pose that Parvati could not do. You will find that pose in the Chidambaram temple, near Chennai in South India. But Parvati could not manage that posture, which became the immortal posture of Nataraja.

After Shiva came Sri Krishna. He brought dance to the level of the masses, to the cowherd boys and girls, who graze and milk the cows. Krishna was illiterate. This man who is supposed to be the master of the *Bhagavad Gita* had no schooling at all, just like Swami Niranjan. Swami Niranjan never went to school; he never knew what a schoolmaster was, or a desk and pen and paper. Krishna had a similar destiny. He never went to school. He lived incognito during his childhood and adolescence with the cowherd boys and girls. There he used to dance and dance and the girls used to dance and dance. That dance has become immortal in

183

Indian history and is called the rasalila, the cosmic dance, the celestial dance, the divine dance. We call it the dance of purusha and prakriti, the dance between ida and pingala. We have given it so many names. Sri Krishna danced and the rasalila has become immortal.

Krishna and Shiva were masters of dancing, they were perfect dancers. Shiva's Nataraja and Krishna's rasalila were missing from Indian life for two or three hundred years, when women and men were not allowed to interact with each other. We are born free. We want to be free. Dancing is our right and singing is our soul. That is the only time when we can be happy. Otherwise we are dancing after money, we are dancing after the bottle, we are dancing after this and that. And that dance is full of tensions.

We do not subscribe to cultures that prohibit singing and dancing. Music and dance are the elixir of life. Everyone must allow their children to learn music and dance at home. We must all learn to sing and dance. See how good these people from the West are at singing and dancing. Their timing and rhythm are perfect. They knowledge is one hundred percent although it is our culture which has come down to us from the *Sama Veda*, one of the four Vedas. During the dark times two to three hundred years ago this gap between boys and girls widened and they were prohibited from practising this beautiful art. As a result today girls and boys are afraid of each other.

We want our children to learn mathematics and science, but life in society and the family should be full of music. There is no harm in learning English or chemistry but children must sing and dance. Dancing and singing develop the body and mind – their spirits will soar. If parents sing kirtans and bhajans, children will also follow suit. If you sit and chant kirtan or Ramayana, your children will definitely sit there with you and participate in that chanting too. This would be the beginning of a very good culture in the family, one in tune with our ancient culture and civilization. Singing and dancing is not a new culture.

Cradle of civilization

India has been the cradle of all civilizations, but today we have almost forgotten our own heritage. Today we are worshipping the kanya kumaris here. You must remember to rear them to be goddesses. May God bless them so they can learn, read, become educated, dance and sing and finally earn their own living so as to take care of their parents too.

The ancient kings, emperors and saints performed many big yajnas on the banks of the rivers Ganga, Yamuna and Mandakini. From these places great cultures developed and prospered. Now we are performing a very small yajna and several thousand people have congregated here. Cultures progressed out of these yajnas mostly in Uttarkhand where sages and seers like Vyasadev, Jabali and Jamdagni were the preceptors. The seats of the ancient culture were in the area of Gangotri and around Badrinath and Tapovan. Most of the saints and sages settled in those areas. You will not find sannyasins settling in South India for higher realization. The majority find their abode in the north, near and above Rishikesh. People go on pilgrimages to the north because most Indians have visualized the Himalayas as being very sacred. Although we lagged behind in the middle period when Indians were not free to follow their own cultural path, the culture and civilization which flourished on the banks of the Ganga and Yamuna was the best, and as such we worship these rivers as goddesses.

In the last fifty to sixty years, since independence, we have been able to practise our own cultural ways. Now our boys and girls are on the right track. The meaning of my discourse is simple. We must tread very cautiously. Because many devilish things have entered our culture. This Ravani culture, which was followed by *asuras,* demons, in ancient times, will have to be culled. We mistakenly treat it as part of our own culture. We want our culture to be Vedic – good and progressive. We should prosper in scientific knowledge, in technology, in financial matters, in politics. In every sphere we should have a progressive mind and discard all that is regressive. We underwent trials and tribulations for nearly

185

two hundred years, but we have tenacity in this country. Otherwise we might also have been backed into a dark corner. Hence this yajna is a very big occasion, it is historic as well as spiritual. That is why I exhort people to visit wherever such a yajna is being performed – you do not need an invitation for that.

Sri Sukta

Now the offering will be given with the chanting of *Sri Sukta,* which is considered to be the oldest *sukta* or hymn in human history. *Sri Sukta* is an invocation from the *Rig Veda,* the oldest Vedic scripture.

> *O mystic Fire, transport unto me Goddess Lakshmi,*
> *who holds the mace of righteousness,*
> *lustrous like gold,*
> *wearing garlands of gold, bright like the sun*
> *and abundant with wealth.*

Now we are chanting and offering oblations to the fire. In Christian and Jewish rites a lamb used to be sacrificed. That is not done now. The lamb is represented by a pumpkin, so a pumpkin is sacrificed. A pumpkin is equivalent to a lamb or a lamb is equal to a pumpkin. That is the final sacrifice.

Their happiness is my happiness

Oh, the people from this circle have now arrived. Most of the houses in and around this area stand locked today as all the inhabitants have arrived to witness this program of welcoming the newly weds. We are going to welcome the brides who have been married between the last Sita Kalyanam and this one. We welcome them as part and parcel of this ashram and akhara. All the members of this Rikhia panchayat are my disciples and every girl is my disciple. I have made each household my household. I am teaching you the theme of Vedanta. It is written as *atmabhava* in Vedanta. This year one hundred new brides have arrived in our panchayat all of whom will be welcomed today.

186

This is the most important program of this akhara and every home and every child has come to participate. The crowd that you see on the road is a witness to this. It is a very important program in the sense that a hundred girls have entered this panchayat as daughters-in-law since the last Sita Kalyanam, one year ago. Today one year is complete. On this day the akhara felicitates their arrival with a gift. This is not an ordinary gift. It contains as much as forty to fifty thousand rupees worth of materials.

The point is this – I am only passing on to them what you have given. It is not mine. It is you who have given it as bhet. *Bhet* is the art of giving and receiving. So they will be receiving as prasad the bhet you have offered. Bhet has been converted into prasad like the monsoon is transformed into rain. You gifted, you offered, and it has been given as prasad. On behalf of the Devi, the pooja is now over. At the culmination of this yajna these daughters-in-law, my daughters-in-law, your daughters-in-law and every wise man's daughters-in-law will be felicitated. May God bless them. May they receive more suitcases, may they receive more money, may they receive more bounty and more prosperity.

The philosophy is very simple. The entire panchayat is my ashram. Every house here is my house. Their pains and pleasures are my own. Their poverty is my poverty and their happiness is my happiness. If anyone is sick it is my ashram inmate who is sick. That is not a social philosophy, it is Vedantic philosophy. You have to see yourself in everyone and you have to see everyone within your own self.

Abhisheka
Adana
Aisvarya
Anusthana
Aradhana
Atani
Avali
Ashrama
Astina
Atma linga
Amabhasa
Avidya
Barti – ......
Bhakta – ...
Bhakti
Bhava Santi ...

Bhavana

Glossary

Abhisheka – ceremonial bathing or anointing of the deity

Akhara – training ground, particularly for sannyasins

Angavastra – man's kurta or shirt

Anushthana – resolve to perform mantra sadhana for a particular period of time with absolute discipline

Aradhana – to be fully immersed in worship of the deity

Arani – piece of wood used in kindling fire by friction during yajna; sacrificial wood

Arati – ceremonial waving of lights

Ashrama – stage or period of life, of which there are four according to the ancient Vedic tradition: brahmacharya (student), grihastha (householder), vanaprastha (retirement) and sannyasa

Asura – demon, enemy of the gods

Atma – the self beyond mind and body; spirit, soul

Atmabhava – feeling yourself in others

Avidya – ignorance

Barfi – sweet prepared from milk or flour of almonds or cashews mixed with ghee

Bhakta – devotee of God

Bhakti – complete devotion to a higher principle of life; love for all beings; devotion as service

Bhava samadhi – absorption in meditation due to emotional cause, i.e. kirtan; superconscious state of existence attained by intense emotion

Bhavana – feeling, emotion; ability to perceive subtle emotions

Bhet – giving

Bhoga – experience of, and craving for, pleasure and enjoyment

Bhramari – breathing practice in which a humming sound is produced like the murmuring of the black bee

Bidi – Indian cigarette wrapped in tobacco leaf

Brahman – ultimate reality

Brahmin – member of the priestly caste

Chakravarti samrat – great monarch

Chandi – the form of Durga who killed the demon Chand

Charkha – spinning wheel

Chitabhoomi – cremation ground

Crore – ten million

Daan – gift

Darshan – real vision; blessing received just by seeing an enlightened or divine being or God

Deoghar – cremation ground of the consort of Shiva in her form as Sati; the main town in Rikhia, where Sri Swamiji presently resides; 'God's house'

Deva – self-luminous being in a male form

Devata – illumined form, divinity that dispels the darkness and reveals the hidden essence

Devi – self-luminous being in a female form

Dwapara Yuga – the second age or yuga of the world

Dwiragaman – traditional farewell ceremony when a bride goes to live in her husband's house for the second and final time

Ganesha – elephant-headed, one-tusked deity; remover of obstacles; symbol of auspiciousness, knowledge and wealth

Gopis – cowherd girls, the transcendental girlfriends of Krishna

Gujhiya – sweet pastry made from flour, condensed milk, dried fruits and ginger, served especially at Holi and Diwali

Havan – fire ceremony

Holi – festival of colours, celebrating the victory of the gods over the demons

Ishq haqiqi – divine love

Ishq mijazi – worldly love

Ishta devata – personal deity

Jalebi – sweet made from gram (chickpea) flour fried in ghee, with saffron and sugar syrup

Jhumaka – long earring of silver or gold

Kali Yuga – current era of the world, difficult and full of strife

Kamsa – maternal uncle of Krishna, demonic king

Kanya – virgin

Karma – action and result

Karmakanda – that part of the Vedas that relates to ceremonial acts and sacrificial rules; daily rituals of worship for a householder

Kheer – sweet prepared from rice, milk, sugar, dried fruits, nuts and spices

Kripa – grace

Krishna – avatar; manifestation of God in human form, eighth incarnation of Lord Vishnu; guru of Arjuna in the Bhagavad Gita; beloved of the gopis

Kshatriya – warrior caste; one who protects others from injury

Laddoo – sweet ball favoured by Ganesha made from gram (chickpea) flour and ghee

Lakh – one hundred thousand

Lakshmi – consort of Lord Vishnu, goddess of prosperity

Langar – serving of free food at a holy place to pilgrims or to the needy

Lehnga-choli – skirt and blouse worn by Indian women

Lila – divine play, pastime; activity of prakriti and its three gunas

Mahabharata – one of the great historical scriptures of India that chronicles the lives and spiritual development of humans, devas, demons, animals and others

Madhuram – sweetness

Maharasa – cosmic experience

Mahatma – great soul

Mandap – decorative thatched roof over the raised platform erected for worship

Mansarovar – the lake of the greater mind

Mantra – sound revealed to sages in deep meditation which liberates the mind from bondage when repeated

Maya – illusory power of creation

Moha – delusion

Moksha – liberation from the wheel of birth and death

Nasha – destruction

Panchagni sadhana – sadhana of the fire fires

Panchayat – village council

Paramartha – the highest service, highest truth or reality

Path – any set of mantras to be chanted

Patra daan – prasad of utensils

Peda – a sweet, like milk fudge, found all over India

Phalgun – Hindu calendar month (March/April)

Pooja – honour, respect; rites; worship

Poornahuti – the final rite in a fire ceremony or yajna where offerings are made to the flames and a wish is made

Pradakshina – walking ceremonially around a revered object

Prakriti – active principle of the manifest world

Prarabdha karma – the portion of karma that determines one's present life

Prasad – blessed object; grace, purity; pleasure, happiness

Puri – fried roti made from flour, water and ghee

Purusha – pure consciousness

Purushartha – personal effort; the four goals to be attained in life: artha, kama, dharma and moksha

Rabadi – sweet made from condensed milk and cream, sprinkled with nuts

Radha – transcendental lover of Krishna, chief of the gopis

Rajadanda – weapon of a ruler

Rajasooya Yajna – sacrifice performed by a king entitled to assume the title of emperor

Rama – hero of the Ramayana, seventh incarnation of Vishnu, the embodiment of dharma

Ramacharitamanas – the story of Lord Rama as a poetic composition written by Goswami Tulsidas

Rasa – a transcendental mellow relationship between the individual soul and the supreme Lord

Rasalila – Krishna's transcendental pastime of dancing with the gopis in Vrindavan; cosmic dance

Ravana – a most powerful demon who threatened the whole earth, abducted Sita and was vanquished by Rama

Rechaka – exhalation

Rishi – Vedic seer

Sakhi – female friend or attendant

Samskara – unconscious memory, mental impression

Sandesh – choice Bengali milk sweet

Sankalpa – positive affirmation, resolve

Sannyasa – dedication; complete renunciation of the world, its possessions and attachments

Santhalis – tribesmen of the region of Santhal, where Rikhia is located

Shankaracharya – the great teacher who revitalized the Shaivite tradition and established the Adwaita Vedanta philosophy; founder of the Dashnami order of sannyasa

Shishupala – enemy of Krishna

Shraddha – reverence

Shyam – a name of Krishna, glorifying his dark complexion

Shiva – supreme consciousness; auspiciousness, lord of the yogis, male principle

Sita – incarnation of shakti as the wife of Rama, kundalini shakti, mother goddess

Srimad Bhagavatam – Vedic text that deals with the pastimes of Krishna and his devotees

Shringara – items of beautification traditionally given to a bride

Sri Yantra – the most respected yantra, symbol of the goddess

Sthapana – the entire installation of the deity in accordance with the sacred rites

Sudarshan chakra – the wheel which is the personal weapon of Vishnu or Krishna

Tabiz – amulet, talisman to ward off evil forces

Tantra – ancient science of inducing spiritual experience, 'expansion and liberation'; esoteric technique leading one from outside into one's own self; one of the six classical Indian philosophies

Thela – push cart

Treta Yuga – the second age or yuga in which Rama incarnated

Tulsidas – author of the Ramacharitamanas

Upasana – personalized form of worship

Vastra daan – prasad of cloth

Vedanta – one of the six systems of Vedic philosophy; 'end of perceivable knowledge'

Vedas – ancient spiritual scriptures: Rig Veda, Yajur Veda, Sama Veda and Atharva Veda

Vinayaka – another name for Ganesha

Vishwas – faith

Yajna – sacrificial rite, offering oblations to the fire

Yantra – geometrical symbol designed for concentration to unleash the hidden potential within the consciousness; visual form of mantra which holds the essence of manifestation; symbol of divinity

Yogadanda – weapon of yoga

Yogamaya – the power of divine illusion

Yudhishthira – eldest of the five Pandava brothers

Yuga – a world cycle, the four being: Satya, Treta, Dwapara and the present Kali

Index

Anusooya 135–136
Atmabhava 24–24, 131, 186–187

Balance 124–125
Bhagavad Gita 40
Bhakti 6, 32, 182–184; See also God
Bhet 6, 187
Bholenath 122–123, 146–152
Bihar Yoga Bharati 82–83, 126, 129

Chandi Yajna 105
Chanting 124–125, 137
Children 74–75; education 108–116
Christ 163–165; in India 59, 165, 176–178
Christianity 59, 176–178
Clapping 48–49
Creation 52–54

Daan 5, 20, 71, 75, 128
Dance 31–32, 50, 183–184; cosmic dance 51
Destiny 17
Devi 60, 84, 86, 139; grace of 13; installation 86
Devotion 27, 148
Diet 61–62
Durga Saptashati 79, 124
Duty, to society 24, 91–92, 110–111, 139–140

Ecology 102–103
Education 112–115; in Rikhia 108–110
Ego 29–30
Energy fields 87–88
Equal opportunity 111–112
Evolution, purpose of 19–20

Freedom 103–104
Friendship 90

Gandhi 77–78, 130–131
Ganesha 137–139
George Harrison 27–28
Gifts 21–22
Girls, and education 112–115
Giving 71–73, 74–75, 92, 94
God 28, 47, 61, 80, 87, 169–170; forms of 41, 52, 56, 65, 170–171; grace of 17–18, 34–36, 120, 159–160; God's name 8, 26–27, 31; See also Bhakti
Good luck kits 155–156
Goodness 136–137

Head, heart and hands 102–103
Holi 63–64
Householders 134–135, 136–137

Independence 93–94
India, and spirituality 176–179, 185–186

195

Ishta devata 117
Karma 17
Kirtan 26, 31
Krishna 28–29, 37–44, 46–47, 50–56, 63, 65, 104–105, 183–184
Kumbha mela 123–124

Love 28

Maharasa 49–54
Mandala 84–85
Mantra 84, 86, 125, 165–166
Marriage 112–115, 133–134, 155–156, 160–161
Mother 60–61, 79
Munger 132–133
Music 16, 30–31, 183–184

Offering 20
Old age 73–74

Panchagni 123, 127
Polytheism 8–9, 41, 47, 65, 169–171, 179
Poverty 24, 140–141
Prasad 21–22, 35, 45, 75, 127, 128–129, 130–131, 138–139, 152–154; distribution 67, 90, 106–107, 108, 113–114, 155–156, 186–187
Prayer 9–11, 105–106
Purusha and prakriti 49–51, 54–55
Purushartha 17, 125

Radha 51, 63
Rajasooya Yajna 1–2, 6–7, 14–15, 58, 62, 69, 71–72, 80, 92, 104, 126–127, 129, 154; diet 61–62; prasad 5, 62, 72,

78, 130–131, 157–159, 162–163, 173–174
Rama and Sita 68–69, 160–161
Ramacharitamanas 137, 173
Rasalila 29, 42–44, 64–66
Reality 61
Resolve, of yajna 67, 88–89, 105–106, 159–160
Rikhia 131–132; children and education 108–110; equal pay 82; newly weds 155–156; prasad distribution 90; Santhalis 81–8, 95–96

Samskara 150
Sannyasins 68, 75, 83–84; duty to society 140, 141–142, 143–145, 174–176; and family life 134–135, 136–137
Santhalis 81–82, 95–96
Selfless service 98–99
Serving others 24–25
Sharing 23–24
Shishupala 104–105
Shiva 55, 183–184
Sita, marriage 160–161
Sita-Rama Vivah 156–157
Sita Kalyanam 155–157
Sivananda Math 144–145
Society; balance in 74–75; duty to 24, 91–92, 110–111, 139–140; load bearers 91–93, 110–111; needs of 142–143
Spirituality and the West 166–167
Sri Yantra 84, 85
Swami Satsangi 144–145
Swami Satyananda; childhood 96–97; education 76–77; God 18–19, 120; God's instrument 171–173; Iran 181–182;

ishta devata 117–120; parivrajaka 98; Rikhia 108–109, 131–132; Rishikesh 69–70, 97, 172; South America 59–60, 165–166, 180–181; spreading yoga 58–60, 69, 75–76, 121, 126–127, 129, 163, 165–167, 180–182; Trayambakeshwar 117–120, 121–122

Tantra 85–86
Theme song 9–11, 88, 105–106

Villagers 90–93, 95–96
Widows 78, 112
Women; education 112–115; equal rights 82, 111–112; marriage 155–157; prasad 15–16

Yajna 2–7, 13–14, 17, 20, 57, 70–71, 74, 86–87, 100–104, 128–129; Chandi Yajna; chanting 57–58, 61, 125–126; diet 61–62; ecology 102–103; poornahuti 154–155, 186; prasad 21–22, 67, 72, 155–157, 173–174; purpose 33, 100–102; Rajasooya Yajna 1–2, 6–7, 14–15, 58, 6, 69, 71–72, 80, 92, 126–127, 129, 154, 157–158, 162–163; resolve 67, 88–89; rules 12–13, 21–22, 32–34
Yantra 84–86
Yogamaya 53

197

INTERNATIONAL YOGA FELLOWSHIP MOVEMENT (IYFM)

The IYFM is a charitable and philosophical movement founded by Swami Satyananda at Rajnandgaon in 1956 to disseminate the yogic tradition throughout the world. It forms the medium to convey the teachings of Swami Satyananda through its affiliated centres around the world. Swami Niranjanananda is the first Paramacharya of the International Yoga Fellowship Movement.

The IYFM provides guidance, systematized yoga training programs and sets teaching standards for all the affiliated yoga teachers, centres and ashrams. A Yoga Charter to consolidate and unify the humanitarian efforts of all sannyasin disciples, yoga teachers, spiritual seekers and well-wishers was introduced during the World Yoga Convention in 1993. Affiliation to this Yoga Charter enables the person to become a messenger of goodwill and peace in the world, through active involvement in various far-reaching yoga-related projects.

BIHAR SCHOOL OF YOGA (BSY)

The Bihar School of Yoga is a charitable and educational institution founded by Swami Satyananda at Munger in 1963, with the aim of imparting yogic training to all nationalities and to provide a focal point for a mass return to the ancient science of yoga. The Chief Patron of Bihar School of Yoga is Swami Niranjanananda. The original school, Sivanandashram, is the centre for the Munger locality. Ganga Darshan, the new school established in 1981, is situated on a historic hill with panoramic views of the river Ganges.

Yoga Health Management, Teacher Training, Sadhana, Kriya Yoga and other specialized courses are held throughout the year. BSY is also renowned for its sannyasa training and the initiation of female and foreign sannyasins.

BSY provides trained sannyasins and teachers for conducting yoga conventions, seminars and lectures tours around the world. It also contains a comprehensive research library and scientific research centre.

SIVANANDA MATH (SM)

Sivananda Math is a social and charitable institution founded by Swami Satyananda at Munger in 1984, in memory of his guru, Swami Sivananda Saraswati of Rishikesh. The Head Office is now situated at Rikhia in Deoghar district, Bihar. Swami Niranjanananda is the Chief Patron.

Sivananda Math aims to facilitate the growth of the weaker and underprivileged sections of society, especially rural communities. Its activities include: distribution of free scholarships, clothing, farm animals and food, the digging of tube-wells and construction of houses for the needy, assistance to farmers in ploughing and watering their fields. The Rikhia complex also houses a satellite dish system for providing global information to the villagers.

A medical clinic has been established for the provision of medical treatment, advice and education. Veterinary services are also provided. All services are provided free and universally to everyone, regardless of caste and creed.

YOGA RESEARCH FOUNDATION (YRF)

The Yoga Research Foundation is a scientific, research-oriented institution founded by Swami Satyananda at Munger in 1984. Swami Niranjanananda is the Chief Patron of the foundation.

YRF aims to provide an accurate assessment of the practices of different branches of yoga within a scientific framework, and to establish yoga as an essential science for the development of mankind. At present the foundation is working on projects in the areas of fundamental research and clinical research. It is also studying the effects of yoga on proficiency improvement in various social projects, e.g. army, prisoners, children. These projects are being carried out in affiliated centres worldwide.

YRF's future plans include literary, scriptural, medical and scientific investigations into other little-known aspects of yoga for physical health, mental well-being and spiritual upliftment.

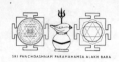

SRI PANCHDASHNAM PARAMAHAMSA ALAKH BARA

SRI PANCHDASHNAM PARAMAHAMSA
ALAKH BARA (PPAB)

Sri Panchdashnam Paramahamsa Alakh Bara was established in 1990 by Swami Satyananda at Rikhia, Deoghar, Bihar. It is a charitable, educational and non-profit making institution aiming to uphold and propagate the highest tradition of sannyasa, namely vairagya (dispassion), tyaga (renunciation) and tapasya (austerity). It propounds the tapovan style of living adopted by the rishis and munis of the vedic era and is intended only for sannyasins, renunciates, ascetics, tapasvis and paramahamsas. The Alakh Bara does not conduct any activities such as yoga teaching or preaching of any religion or religious concepts. The guidelines set down for the Alakh Bara are based on the classical vedic tradition of sadhana, tapasya and swadhyaya, or atma chintan.

Swami Satyananda, who resides permanently at the Alakh Bara, has performed the Panchagni Vidya and other vedic sadhanas, thus paving the way for future paramahamsas to uphold their tradition.

बिहार योग भारती
BIHAR YOGA BHARATI

BIHAR YOGA BHARATI (BYB)

Bihar Yoga Bharati was founded by Swami Niranjanananda in 1994 as an educational and charitable institution for advanced studies in yogic sciences. It is the culmination of the vision of Swami Sivananda and Swami Satyananda. BYB is the world's first government accredited university wholly devoted to teaching yoga. A comprehensive yogic education is imparted with provision to grant higher degrees in yogic studies such as MA, MSc, MPhil, DLitt, and PhD to the students. It offers a complete scientific and yogic education according to the needs of today, through the faculties of Yoga Philosophy, Yoga Psychology, Applied Yogic Science and Yogic Ecology.

Residential courses of four months to two years are conducted in a gurukul environment, so that along with yoga education, the spirit of seva (selfless service), samarpan (dedication) and karuna (compassion) for humankind is also imbibed by the students.

YOGA PUBLICATIONS TRUST (YPT)

Yoga Publications Trust (YPT) was established by Swami Niranjan-ananda in 2000. It is an organization devoted to the dissemination and promotion of yogic and allied knowledge – psychology (ancient and modern), ecology, medicine, vedic, upanishadic, tantric darshanas, philosophies (Eastern and Western), mysticism and spirituality – nationally and internationally through the distribution of books, magazines, audio and video cassettes and multimedia.

YPT is primarily concerned with publishing textbooks in the areas of yoga philosophy, psychology and applied yogic science, research materials, practice texts and the inspiring talks of eminent spiritual personalities and authors aimed at the upliftment of humanity by means of the eternal yogic knowledge, lifestyle and practice.